Geological Association of Canada
Mineral Deposits Division

ORE MINERAL ATLAS

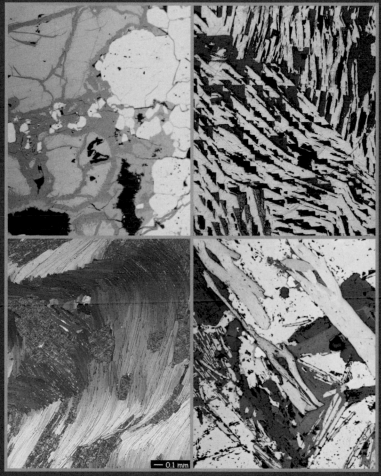

— 0.1 mm

Dan Marshall, C.D. Anglin and Hamid Mumin

 SIMON FRASER

 BRANDON UNIVERSITY
Founded 1899

 CANADA
1842
GEOLOGICAL SURVEY - COMMISSION GÉOLOGIQUE

Geological Association of Canada
Mineral Deposits Division

ORE MINERAL ATLAS

Dan Marshall, C. D. Anglin and Hamid Mumin

Mineral Deposits Division Series Editor
Dirk Tempelman-Kluit

Mineral Deposits Division Steering Committee
John Jambor, Art Soregaroli, Ross Beaty, Bob Cathro and Dirk Tempelman-Kluit

Special Contributors
Holly Keyes, Peter Adamo and Danae Voormeij

Contributors:

Aichmeier, Adolf	McCandless, Tom
Anderson, Alan	McKay, Nicki
Armstrong, John	Perrin, Jonathon
Beaty, Ross	Plumb, Wilfrid
Beaudoin, Georges	Poulin, Roger
Couëslan, Chris	Ramik, Bob
Day, Kerry	Roussy, Jonathon
Gulliver, Austin	Schroeter, Tom
Hamilton, John	Simandl, George
Hanley, Jacob	Sinclair, Dave
Hubbard, Laura	Smith, Moira
Huot, François	Soregaroli, Art
Jonasson, Ian	Twaites, Lloyd
Katchen, Jerry	van Hees, Ed
Lentz, Dave	Watkinson, Dave
Lightfoot, Peter	Wilson, Graham
Mauthner, Mark	

Final Layout: Elizabeth Ambrose

The pictures on the front cover are photomicrographs from the digenite, galena, hematite and molybdenite sections.

The specimen of gold on the back cover is approximately 5 cm tall and is from the Eagle's Nest mine, Placer County, California. Ross Beaty Collection. Photograph by Mark Mauthner.

National Library of Canada Cataloguing in Publication Data

Main entry under title:
Ore Mineral Atlas / Dan Marshall, C.D. Anglin, and Hamid Mumin- 2nd ed.
ISBN 978-0-86491-318-0

Geological Association of Canada, Mineral Deposits Division - L'Association géologique du Canada, Division des gites minéraux
Includes bibliographic references and index

1. Minerals - Identification   2. Ores - Identification
I. Marshall, Daniel D. (1959-) II. Anglin, Carolyn Diane (1959-)   III. Mumin, A. Hamid (1954-)
IV. Geological Association of Canada Mineral Deposits Division   V. Title.
QE390.M37 2004   553   C2004-902030-7

Publisher
Geological Association of Canada - Mineral Deposits Division
Department of Earth Sciences
Room ER4063, Alexander Murray Building
Memorial University of Newfoundland
St. John's, Newfoundland, Canada A1B 3X5
Phone (709) 737-7660; Fax (709) 737-2532
E-mail gac@esd.mun.ca Website www.gac.ca

Printed and bound in Canada by Friesens Corporation

The GEOLOGICAL ASSOCIATION OF CANADA (GAC) is Canada's national society for the geosciences. It was established in 1947 to advance geology and its understanding among both professionals and the general public. The GAC membership of about 2500 includes representatives of all geological disciplines from across Canada and many parts of the world. It has specialist divisions for environmental earth sciences, geophysics, marine geosciences, mineral deposits, paleontology, Precambrian, sedimentology, structural geology and tectonics, volcanology and igneous petrology, remote sensing, geomorphology, and geographic information systems. Regional sections of GAC have been set up in Victoria, Vancouver, Edmonton, Winnipeg and St. John's, and there are affiliated groups in Canada and the United States.

   GAC activities include the organization and sponsorship of conferences, seminars, short courses, field trips, lecture tours and student and professional awards and grants. The Association publishes the quarterly journal *Geoscience Canada* and the quarterly newsletter GEOLOG, a Special Paper series, Short Course Notes and several continuing series. GAC also maintains liaison with other earth science societies and provides advice to government and the public on geological issues. The Association was incorporated under the Canada Corporations Act in January 1984.

   For information contact: Geological Association of Canada, Department of Earth Sciences, Memorial University of Newfoundland, St. John's, Newfoundland, Canada A1B 3X5; E-mail gac@esd.mun.ca Internet site: www.gac.ca.

L'ASSOCIATION GÉOLOGIQUE DU CANADA (AGC) est la société nationale canadienne des sciences de la Terre. Elle a été fondée en 1947 dans le but de contribuer à l'avancement de la géologie et de sensibiliser le grand public aux sciences de la Terre. Elle comprend environ 2500 membres, représentant toutes les disciplines géologiques et provenant de toutes les régions du Canada et d'ailleurs dans le monde. L'AGC comprend des divisions spécialisées en géologie de l'environnement, géophysique, géologie marine, gisements minéraux, paléontologie, géologie du Précambrien, sédimentologie, géologie structurale, tectonique, volcanologie et pétrologie ignée, télédetection, géomorphologie et systèmes d'information géographique. Des sections régionales ont été établies à Victoria, Vancouver, Edmonton, Winnipeg et Saint-Jean (Terre Neuve), et il existe des groupes affiliés au Canada et aux Etats-Unis.

   Les activités de l'AGC comprennent l'organisation et le parrainage de conférences, de colloques, d'ateliers, d'excursions de terrain, de tournées de conférences et l'attribution de distinctions honorifiques pour étudiants et professionnels. L'Association publie le journal trimestriel *Geoscience Canada*, le bulletin d'information trimestriel *GEOLOG*, une série de volumes spéciaux, des notes d'ateliers et d'autres séries de publications. L'AGC maintient en outre des liens avec d'autres sociétés en sciences de la Terre et agit à titre de conseillère auprès des gouvernements et du public sur des questions d'intérêt géologique. L'Association a été incorporée en janvier 1984 en vertu de la Loi sur les corporations canadiennes.

   Pour de plus amples renseignements, veuillez communiquer avec : L'Association géologique du Canada, Department of Earth Sciences, Memorial University of Newfoundland, St. John's, Newfoundland, Canada A1B 3X5; Courriel: gac@esd.mun.ca; Site internet : www.gac.ca.

PREFACE AND ACKNOWLEDGMENTS

Initial discussions regarding the publication of an Ore Mineral Atlas began in 1999. Jason Dunning, then the president of the Mineral Deposits Division and a keen student of ore deposits, thought that there was a need for a simple atlas of ore minerals that would serve as a field reference guide for working geologists and students. Our subsequent years spent in the classroom have reinforced the need for this book. A great debt of thanks is owed to the students who suffered through optical mineralogy labs without this atlas. Our students were fundamental in drawing attention to required contents, in finding mineral specimens, textures or optical properties worthy of photographing, and in some cases researching information on the optical properties or the environment of formation of some minerals.

We would like to acknowledge the invaluable help of the Mineral Deposits Division publications director (Dirk Tempelman-Kluit), and the Steering Committee comprised of Ross Beaty, Bob Cathro, John Jambor, Art Soregaroli, and Dirk Templeman-Kluit. Much of the material contained in this atlas was solicited from the ore-deposits community. Art Soregaroli worked tirelessly to supply us with the final specimens, photos, and thin sections we needed. He dug through the Teck Cominco files for old polished-section pictures, and contacted other collectors for material. With Art's help we have photographed more than a hundred specimens.

Danae Voormeij worked with tireless enthusiasm helping to compile data, suggest additions, and truly moved the atlas along in its early stages. Holly Keyes, field assistant at Simon Fraser, contributed some knowledge of desktop publishing, a keen photographic eye, and an interest in ore minerals. Holly generously gave up large portions of her free time to help in the final stages. Peter Adamo, award-winning photographer and Instructional Associate at Brandon University, combined geological and artistic talents to contribute some excellent photographs. Tania Jurca fought her way through the perils of desktop publishing in Quark Express and got the atlas to the stage that we could hand it off to Elizabeth Ambrose, who kindly provided the final layout and finishing touches.

Last, but certainly not least, are the many individuals who contributed samples, thin sections, and photographs. These persons are listed individually with their affiliations in the figure captions. The atlas would not have been possible without these contributions. We are very grateful to Drs. Moira Smith and Jim Franklin for their very thorough reviews and excellent suggestions for additions to the text. We would also like to acknowledge financial support from the Geological Survey of Canada (Natural Resources Canada) to assist in the printing of this volume.

Dan Marshall

C.D. ('Lyn) Anglin

Hamid Mumin

TABLE OF CONTENTS
(alphabetically)

TABLE OF CONTENTS
(by chemical grouping)

INTRODUCTION

Hand-specimen identification and optical mineralogy are two of the most important tools of the ore-deposit geologist, and there is little available in the way of reference material for students who are trying to learn these skills. Although excellent books (Ramdohr, 1980; Craig and Vaughn, 1981; 1994; Picot, 1982; Uytenbogaardt and Burke, 1985; Ixer, 1991; Picot and Johan, 1991) have been available, they invariably go out of print, are priced well beyond the means of the average student, or are too detailed and expensive to have in the field or around the microscopy lab. Numerous internet resources are also available, but not always convenient to access. This atlas, containing information on ore mineral properties and illustrative photographs, aims to augment these excellent resources by providing a relatively simple, inexpensive reference that can be used (and taken) anywhere, by everyone from undergraduate students to practicing exploration geologists.

This volume illustrates and describes fifty-three of the most common economic ore minerals. Information for this atlas has been compiled from a number of sources, most notably Picot and Johan (1991), Craig and Vaughn (1994), Hurlburt and Klein (1977), Ford (1932), www.galleries.com, and www.webmineral.com. Additionally, the layout of this atlas draws heavily on the GAC Mineral Deposits Division Atlas of Alteration (Thompson and Thompson, 1996).

The minerals and their corresponding page numbers are listed in the two tables of contents. Minerals are listed in alphabetical order in the first table and by chemical group in the second. All minerals are also listed in the index at the back of the book. The page number in bold in the index refers to the primary page for each mineral. Additional page numbers refer to text or images where other references to a mineral occur.

Mineral abbreviations are sometimes ambiguous. Those used here attempt to strike a balance between the abbreviations of Kretz (1983), Chace (1956), common usage, and the abbreviations from the mineralogy website of the University of Geneva. Abbreviations are listed in lower case to avoid confusion between native elements and their chemical symbols.

Colours of the minerals and the polished/thin section images differ. This may result from lighting conditions, mineral compositions, degree of weathering, individual microscope equipment, film type, and cameras utilized. As the images used in this atlas are from different sources, the colours may be difficult to reproduce. Every effort has been made to ensure colour fidelity.

Each mineral is presented on facing pages. The mineral, chemical formula, abbreviation, environment of formation, and crystal system are listed at the top of the left page. The environment of formation refers to the most common ore-forming environment(s) for the mineral. Most minerals occur in a variety of these settings, and we have limited the list to general ore-forming environments such as placer, vein, epithermal, magmatic, porphyry, skarn, secondary, supergene, sedimentary exhalative (SEDEX), volcanogenic massive sulphide (VMS), mesothermal (also referred to as orogenic), pegmatite, carbonatite, metamorphic, intrusion-related, sedimentary, hot spring, iron-oxide-copper-gold (IOCG), and Mississippi Valley type (MVT). For more information on mineral deposit models and environments of ore formation, readers are referred to several excellent references including; Eckstrand (1984), Guilbert and Park (1986), Roberts and Sheahan (1988) and Eckstrand et al. (1995).

Hand-specimen colour, hardness, and density (g/cc) are tabulated along with polished-section colour, bireflectance, anisotropism, cleavage, and reflectivity (Refl). Reflectivity is used to describe the percentage of light reflected from the polished surface of the mineral. Numerous reflectivity datasets exist. Those reported here are interpolated from the data of Picot and Johan (1991). Reflectivity varies as a function of wavelength, polish, and equipment. Colours for the anisotropy of the minerals are reported under partly to fully crossed polars. Bireflectance refers to the colour change observed during stage rotation in plane-polarized reflected light.

Distinguishing features, associated minerals, modes of occurrence, and references for each mineral are also listed. The latter generally include a mineralogical reference, one with pictures or descriptions of the mineral, and another for specific ore-deposit types for the mineral.

For most minerals, four images of the mineral are presented on the right page: two hand specimen photos and two polished or thin-section photos. The photos submitted by individuals have been reviewed by the authors and steering committee. Every attempt has been made to include "real" as opposed to "museum specimen" pictures of minerals showing typical characteristics and associated minerals. The polished thin-section photos are chosen to emphasize features visible in reflected light, most notably colour, anisotropism, and textures.

The Determinative Mineral Guide (after Spry and Gedlinske, 1987) can be used as a quick logical guide to rapidly identify the major species within this atlas based on colour, bireflectance, isotropy, transmissivity (internal reflectivity) and hardness. The hardness is based on a relative scale of soft, medium, and hard and is generally observable as scratches in the soft minerals and as doming or relief in the harder minerals. Some minerals display variable characteristics and may appear more than once in the determinative table.

References:

Chace F.M. (1956) Abbreviations in field and mine geological mapping. Economic Geology, v. 51, p. 712-723.

Craig J.R. and Vaughn D.J. (1981) Ore Microscopy and Ore Petrography. John Wiley and sons, New York, 406 p.

Craig J.R. and Vaughn D.J. (1994) Ore Microscopy and Ore Petrography, 2nd Edition. John Wiley and sons, New York, 434 p.

Deer W.A., Howie R.A. and Zussman J. (1992) An Introduction to the Rock-Forming Minerals, 2nd edition. Longman, Hong Kong, 696 p.

Eckstrand O.R. (1984) Canadian Mineral Deposit Types: A Geological Synopsis. Geological Survey of Canada, Economic Geology Report 36, Canadian Government Publishing Centre, 86 p.

Eckstrand O.R., Sinclair W.D, and Thorpe R.I. (1995) Geology of Canadian Mineral Deposit Types. Geological Survey of Canada, Geology of Canada No. 8, 640 p.

Ford W.E. (1932) Dana's Textbook of Mineralogy, 4th edition. Wiley and sons, New York. 851 p.

Guilbert J.M. and Park C.F. Jr. (1986) The Geology of Ore Deposits. W.H. Freeman and Company, New York, 985 p.

Hurlburt C.S. and Klein C. (1977) Manual of Mineralogy, 19th Edition. John Wiley and sons, New York, 532 p.

Ixer R.A. (1991) Atlas of Opaque and Ore Minerals in their Associations. Van Nostrand Reinhold, New York. 208 p.

Kretz R. (1983) Symbols for rock-forming minerals. American Mineralogist, v. 68, p. 277-279.

Picot P. and Johan Z. (1991) Atlas of Ore Minerals. Translated from the original French version: Atlas des minéraux métalliques: Picot P. (1982). Elsevier, Amsterdam. 458 p.

Ramdohr P. (1980) The Ore Minerals and their Intergrowths. Pergamon Press, Oxford, UK. 1205 p.

Roberts R.G. and Sheahan P.A. (1988) Ore Deposit Models. Geoscience Canada, Reprint Series 3, Geological Association of Canada, 194 p.

Spry P. and Gedlinkse B. (1987) Tables for the determination of opaque minerals: Economic Geology Publishing Company, 54 p.

Thompson A.J.B. and Thompson J.F.H (1996) Atlas of Alteration, a Field and Petrographic Guide to Hydrothermal Alteration Minerals. Geological Association of Canada Publication. 119 p.

Uytenbogaardt W. and Burke E.A.J. (1985) Tables for Microscopic Identification of Ore Minerals, 2nd edition. Dover Publications, New York, 430 p.

MINERAL IDENTIFICATION GUIDE

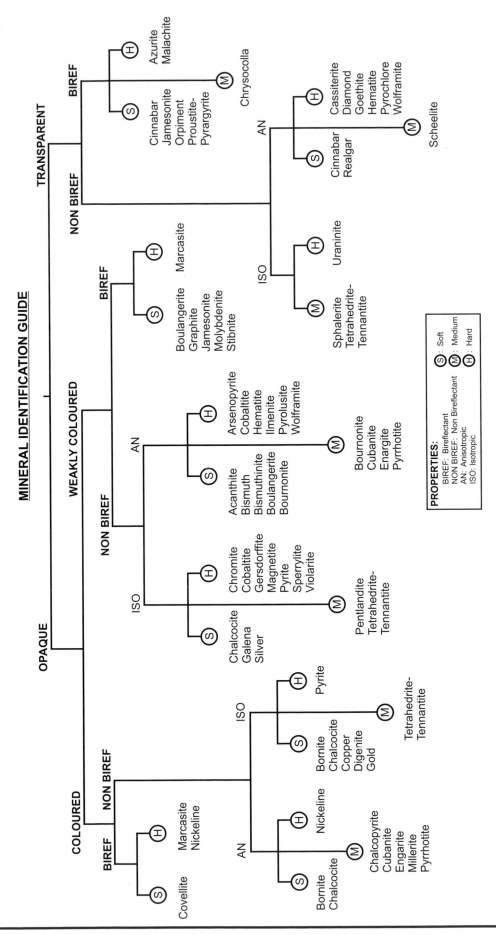

PROPERTIES:
BIREF: Bireflectant
NON BIREF: Non Bireflectant
AN: Anisotropic
ISO: Isotropic

S : Soft
M : Medium
H : Hard

ORE FORMING MINERALS

Acanthite (aca)

Environment: Epithermal, vein

Ag_2S

Monoclinic (Pseudocubic)

Characteristics

Hand Specimen	
Colour	Metallic black to grey
Hardness	2 – 2½
Density	7.2 – 7.4

Polished Section			
Colour	Grey, slightly greenish	Cleavage	{0001} Imperfect
Bireflectance	Very weak	Anisotropy	Distinct: bluish-grey
Refl (546nm)	30.6 – 32.6	Refl (589nm)	29.4 – 31.2

Distinguishing Features

Acanthite in hand specimen is lead-grey to iron-black with metallic lustre (which tarnishes to dark grey with a dull lustre) and a shiny black streak. It has a high specific gravity, is soft and sectile. Crystal habit may be pseudo-cubic or pseudo-orthorhombic after argentite (see below). Lower temperature forms are slender prismatic or skeletal crystals, or occur as coatings. In polished section, it is grey with a greenish tint, has low reflectance, very weak bireflectance but distinct anisotropy when well polished. However, it is difficult to polish due to its softness.

Associated Minerals

A significant ore of silver, acanthite occurs with native silver and other silver-bearing minerals such as proustite, pyrargyrite, stephanite, polybasite and also galena, tetrahedrite, fluorite, and cobalt-nickel ores.

Mode of Occurrence

Acanthite is generally a low-temperature hydrothermal mineral commonly occurring in vein deposits (e.g. Cobalt and Thunder Bay) and the epithermal environment. Commonly seen as irregular inclusions in galena, acanthite also occurs as anhedral polycrystalline aggregates or as euhedral cubic pseudomorphs after argentite. Note: all Ag_2S at room temperature is acanthite. Argentite is the higher temperature polymorph of Ag_2S, which is stable above 177°C.

References

Franklin J.M. (1970) Metallogeny of the Proterozoic Rocks of Thunder Bay District, Ontario. PhD. thesis, University of Western Ontario, London, Ontario, 318 p.

Greiffé C., Bailly L. and Milesi J-P. (2002) Supergene alteration of primary ore assemblages from low-sulphidation Au-Ag epithermal deposits at Pongkor, Indonesia, and Nazareño, Perú. Economic Geology, v. 97, p. 561-571.

Kracek F.C. (1946) Phase relations in the system silver-sulfur and the transitions in silver sulfide. Transactions of the American Geophysical Union, v. 27, 367-374.

Petruk W. and staff (1971) Characteristics of the sulphides. Canadian Mineralogist, v. 11, 196-231.

Petruk W., Owens D.R., Stewart J.M. and Murray, E.J. (1974) Observations on acanthite, aguilarite and naumannite. Canadian Mineralogist, v. 12, p. 365-369.

Figures

aca 1 Specimen of a calcite-acanthite-quartz vein that cut Precambrian metasedimentary rocks from the Echo Bay deposit, Port Radium, Northwest Territories. The calcite has been dissolved in acid. Sample from Art Soregaroli.

aca 2 Acanthite with clear to cloudy calcite crystals. There are at least three generations of calcite in this specimen. One predates the acanthite, another is contemporaneous with the acanthite, and a third generation cuts the acanthite. Beaverdell, British Columbia. Sample T1000 from Art Soregaroli. Photograph by Dan Marshall.

aca 3 Acanthite (aca), pyrite (py), and chalcopyrite (cp) in polished thin section from an epithermal deposit hosted in silicate gangue. The sample is from the Simon Fraser University collection. Note the characteristic poor polish on the acanthite. Photo taken in plane polarized reflected light.

aca 4 Photomicrograph showing the same field of view as aca 3 under partly crossed polars. Note the characteristic bluish-grey anisotropic colours of the acanthite on the lower portion of the grain.

Photographs by Dan Marshall.

aca 1

aca 2

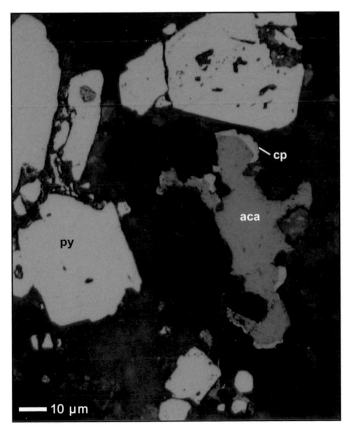

aca 3

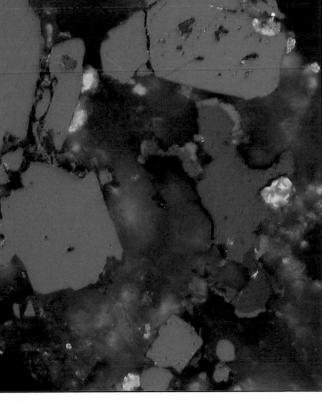

aca 4

Arsenopyrite (apy)

Environment: Magmatic, vein, mesothermal, skarn

FeAsS

Monoclinic

Characteristics

Hand Specimen	
Colour	Silvery white, tarnishes to pink-brown
Hardness	5½ – 6
Density	6.1+

Polished Section			
Colour	White	Cleavage	{110} Good
Bireflectance	Weak	Anisotropy	Strong; blue, green
Refl (546nm)	49.9 – 51.9	Refl (589nm)	50.6 – 51.1

Distinguishing Features

Silvery white colour, striated faces, metallic lustre tarnishing to iridescent pink-brown shades, dark grey to black streak, and high specific gravity. It commonly exhibits prismatic crystal habit with diamond cross-section and twinning. It has a garlic or bitter smell when powdered or broken. In polished section, white colour, strong anisotropism, good polish and rhombic crystal form are characteristic. Anisotropism distinguishes it from pyrite.

Associated Minerals

Commonly associated with hydrothermal gold; also with vein ores of Sn and W in high-temperature hydrothermal deposits. It is also associated with Ag and Cu ores, galena, sphalerite, pyrite, and chalcopyrite. Occurs sparingly in pegmatite, in contact-metamorphic deposits, and in metamorphosed clastic sedimentary rocks.

Mode of Occurrence

Arsenopyrite is the most common As-bearing mineral. It typically occurs as euhedral to subhedral crystals with characteristic rhomb shape or prismatic form (see photo mrc 4). It is commonly twinned, and also occurs as anhedral granular masses where abundant. Arsenopyrite is a widespread mineral in many localities, and in a wide variety of hydrothermal mineral deposits, among which are: the Sn ores in Cornwall, England; the Sn-W veins at Panasqueira, Portugal; the Archean gold veins in Val d'Or, Quebec and Yellowknife, Northwest Territories; in the silver veins at Cobalt, Ontario; and the iron formation-hosted gold deposits at Homestake, South Dakota and Lupin, Northwest Territories.

References

Choi S.-G. and Youm S.-J. (2000) Compositional variation of arsenopyrite and fluid evolution at the Ulsan deposit, southeastern Korea: a low-sulfidation porphyry system. Canadian Mineralogist, v. 38, p. 567-584.

Fleet M.E. and Mumin A.H (1997) Gold-bearing arsenian pyrite and marcasite and arsenopyrite from Carlin Trend gold deposits and laboratory synthesis. American Mineralogist, v. 82, p. 182-193.

Hein K.A.A. (2003) The Batman and Quigleys gold deposits of the Mt. Todd (Yimuyn Manjerr) Mine, Australia: structural, petrographic and mineralogical investigations of coeval quartz sulphide vein and lode/stockwork systems. Ore Geology Reviews, v. 23, p. 3-33.

Kretschmar U. and Scott S.D. (1976) Phase relations involving arsenopyrite in the system Fe-As-S and their application. Canadian Mineralogist, v. 14, p. 364-386.

Lentz D.R. (2002) Sphalerite and arsenopyrite at the Brunswick No. 12 massive-sulfide deposit, Bathurst Camp, New Brunswick; constraints on P-T evolution. Canadian Mineralogist, v. 40, p. 19-31.

Lynch G. and Mengel F. (1995) Metamorphism of arsenopyrite-pyrite-sphalerite-pyrrhotite lenses, western Cape Breton Island, Nova Scotia. Canadian Mineralogist, v. 33, p. 105-114.

Morimoto N. and Clark L.A. (1961) Arsenopyrite crystal-chemical relations. American Mineralogist, v. 46, p. 1448-1469.

Figures

apy 1 Arsenopyrite crystals on quartz from the Sunrise property, Hazelton, British Columbia. Specimen S67.98 from Art Soregaroli.

apy 2 Hand specimen with arsenopyrite crystals (silver) in a cummingtonite schist from the Homestake deposit, South Dakota. Coin diameter is 2.8 cm. Simon Fraser University collection.

apy 3 Photomicrograph of arsenopyrite with rim of pyrrhotite (yellow) Plane polarized reflected light.

apy 4 Same specimen as in **apy 3** taken under partly crossed nicols.

Photographs by Dan Marshall.

apy 1

apy 2

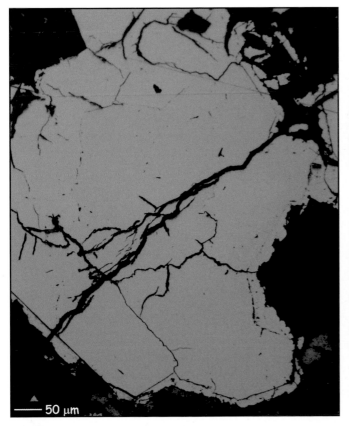

apy 3

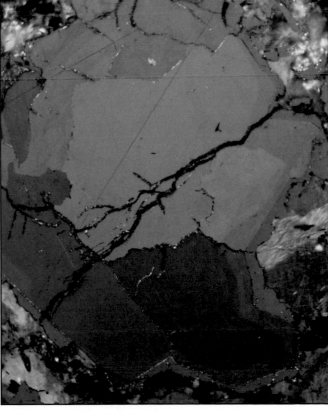

apy 4

Asbestos (asb)

Environment: Secondary, metamorphic

$Mg_3Si_2O_5(OH)_4$

Monoclinic

Characteristics

Hand Specimen	
Colour	White, grey, green, yellow or brown
Hardness	2½ – 3
Density	2.2 – 2.6

Polished Section			
Colour	Colourless to pale green	Cleavage	Fibrous
Bireflectance	–	Anisotropy	–
Refl (546nm)	–	Refl (589nm)	–

Note:

The word asbestos is not a mineral name, but a mineral habit, and a general term applied to some fibrous minerals that have a varied mineralogical and chemical composition. The fibrous minerals termed 'asbestos' may be a serpentine (chrysotile and lizardite) or amphiboles (crocidolite, anthophyllite, tremolite, and actinolite). Chrysotile, the only fibrous species belonging to the serpentine group, is the most important commercial source of asbestos, and is the only asbestos mineral mined in Canada.

Distinguishing Features

Chrysotile asbestos is non-metallic and translucent. The softness, colour, waxy luster, and silky feel result from the parallel, fine fibres. The flexibility of the fibres is a distinctive feature of asbestos.

Associated Minerals

Serpentine, magnetite, chromite, olivine, talc, and other minerals found in serpentinized ultramafic rocks.

Mode of Occurrence

Chrysotile asbestos is formed in peridotitic rocks that have been variably serpentinized. When found in veins of silky fibres, it may be an important commercial source of asbestos. Chrysotile forms during deformation and alteration of ultramafic rocks under low-grade metamorphic conditions (Duke, 1996).

References

Cogulu E. and Laurent R. (1983) Mineralogical and chemical variations in chrysotile veins and peridotite host-rocks from the asbestos belt of southern Quebec. Canadian Mineralogist, v. 22, p. 173-183.

Duke J.M. (1986) Petrology and Economic Geology of the Dumont Sill: An Archean Intrusion of Komatiitic Affinity in Northwestern Quebec. Geological Survey of Canada, Economic Geology Report 35, 56 p.

Duke J.M. (1996) Ultramafic-hosted asbestos. *in* Geology of Canadian Mineral Deposit Types, (ed.) O.R. Eckstrand, W.D. Sinclair, and R.I. Thorpe. Geological Survey of Canada, Geology of Canada No. 8, p. 263-268.

Glen R.A. and Butt B.C. (1981) Chrysotile asbestos at Woodsreef, New South Wales. Economic Geology, v. 76, p. 1153-1169.

O'Hanley D.S. and Wicks F.J. (1995) Conditions of formation of lizardite, chrysotile and antigorite, Cassiar, British Columbia. Canadian Mineralogist, v. 33, p. 753-773.

Wicks, F.J. and O'Hanley, D.S (1988) Serpentine minerals; structures and petrology. *in* Hydrous Phyllosilicates. Mineralogical Society of America, Reviews in Mineralogy, v. 19, p. 91-167.

Figures

asb 1 Chrysotile veins filling fractures in serpentinized ultramafic rock from the Cassiar Asbestos deposit, Cassiar, British Columbia. Photograph by Wilfrid Plumb.

asb 2 Simple (0.5 inch) and complex (smaller) chrysotile veins filling fractures in serpentine. Cassiar Asbestos Mine, open pit. Knife for scale. Photograph by Wilfrid Plumb

asb 3 Lizardite with hour glass texture and spinel (spi). Mont Chagnon, Quebec. F.O.V. 1 mm, plane polarized light under crossed nicols. Photograph by Francois Huot.

asb 4 Chrysotile fibers in vein. Mont Chagnon, Quebec. F.O.V. 3 mm, plane polarized light under crossed nicols. Photograph by Francois Huot.

asb 1

asb 2

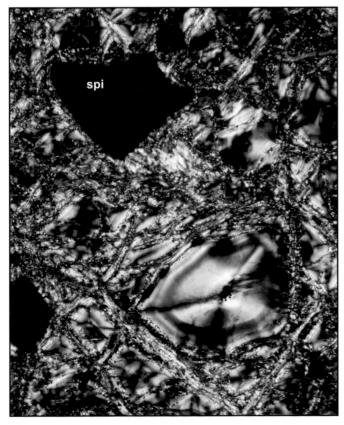

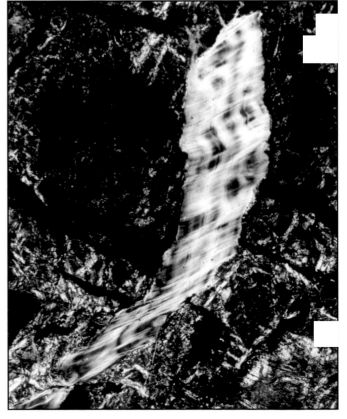

asb 3

asb 4

Azurite (az)

$Cu_3(OH)_2(CO_3)_2$ **Monoclinic**

Characteristics

Hand Specimen	
Colour	Azure blue
Hardness	3½ – 4
Density	3.7 – 3.8

Polished Section			
Colour	Blue	**Cleavage**	{011} Perfect, {100} Imperfect
Bireflectance	Moderate to absent	**Anisotropy**	Strong
Refl (546nm)	Low	**Refl (589nm)**	Low

Distinguishing Features

The azure blue colour and lighter blue streak are distinctive. The lustre is vitreous to dull depending on crystal habit, which varies from euhedral bladed crystals to botryoidal, nodular, and massive forms. In polished section, it is grey, takes a good polish, and has strong anisotropism. Deep blue internal reflections are also characteristic of azurite. In transmitted light, its strong purple to blue pleochroism is diagnostic. It also effervesces in dilute HCl.

Associated Minerals

Commonly associated with the distinctly green coloured malachite. It is also associated with native copper, cuprite, chalcopyrite, chalcocite, bornite, chrysocolla, and other oxidized Cu-bearing minerals.

Mode of Occurrence

Azurite is of secondary origin, occurring in oxidized portions of Cu-bearing ore deposits. It is formed by the reaction of carbon dioxide and water with copper sulphide or by Cu-bearing solutions with carbonate and forms blocky to tabular crystals, slender prismatic crystals, nodular botryoidal masses, and stalactitic and stalagmitic aggregates. It is an important mineral in supergene-weathered deposits such as Cu-porphyry, VMS, and IOCG.

References

Graeme Richard W. (1997) The supergene copper minerals of Bisbee, Arizona. Mineralogical Record. v. 28, p. 55.

Melchiorre E.B., Criss R.E. and Rose T.P. (2000) Oxygen and carbon isotope study of natural and synthetic azurite. Economic Geology, v. 95, p. 621-628.

Sillitoe R.H. (2003) Iron oxide-copper-gold deposits: an Andean view. Mineralium Deposita, v. 38, p. 787-813.

Wilson M.L. (1995) Copper and cuprite pseudomorphs after azurite from the rose mine, Grant County, New Mexico. Annals of Carnegie Museum, v. 64, p. 35-50.

Figures

az 1   Azurite (blue) intergrown with limonite and minor malachite (green) weathered horizon, Bisbee, Arizona. F.O.V. ~2.9 cm x 3.6 cm.

az 2   Drusy to powdery azurite (blue) with iron oxide (brown) and minor malachite (green), weathered horizon, Bisbee, Arizona. F.O.V. ~1.0 cm x 1.3 cm.

az 3   Photomicrograph of azurite showing a range of light to dark blue pleochroism and green amorphous malachite. Polished thin section, plane polarized transmitted light. F.O.V. ~0.34 mm X 0.43 mm.

az 4   Botryoidal azurite (light blue) with drusy coating of azurite crystals (dark blue), weathered horizon, Bisbee, Arizona. F.O.V. ~2.9 cm X 3.6 cm.

Photographs submitted by P.J. Adamo and A.H. Mumin, Brandon University.

az 1

az 2

az 3

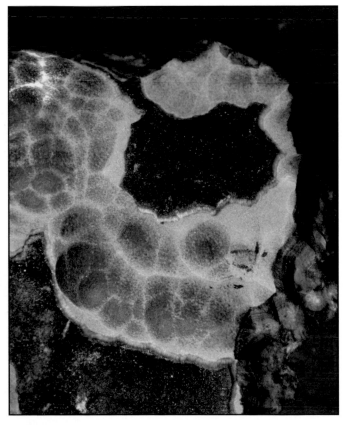

az 4

Bismuth (bi)

Environment: Vein, skarn, magmatic, mesothermal, IOCG, pegmatite

Bi

Trigonal

Characteristics

Hand Specimen	
Colour	Silver-white, when fresh, tarnishing red
Hardness	2 – 2½
Density	9.8

Polished Section			
Colour	White to creamy	Cleavage	{0001} Perfect
Bireflectance	Weak but distinct	Anisotropy	Distinct
Refl (546nm)	63.0 – 64.2	Refl (589nm)	65.4 – 66.8

Distinguishing Features

Native bismuth is distinguished in hand specimen by its hardness, silvery white colour with a reddish tarnish, and silvery white streak, twinning and perfect cleavage. It is brittle but becomes somewhat malleable when heated. In polished section, colour is creamy white with a distinct greenish anisotropism, both of which become reddish with tarnishing. The anisotropism may also be masked by polishing scratches. Bismuth is highly reflective. It is also slightly more yellow than silver, though in fine grains the two minerals can appear quite similar.

Associated Minerals

A comparatively rare mineral, bismuth occurs with ores of Au, Ag, Co, Ni, Cu, Zn, Pb, and Sn. It occurs with sulphosalts, sphalerite, chalcopyrite, wolframite, arsenopyrite, cassiterite, molybdenite, galena, and pyrite.

Mode of Occurrence

Bismuth occurs as irregular masses or inclusions of anhedral crystals. It occurs in pegmatite and also in silver veins, for example in small veins associated with silver and cobalt minerals at Cobalt, Canada and in minor amounts in the silver veins in the Thunder Bay area. Commonly associated with types of igneous intrusion-related hydrothermal deposits, such as the Sn-ore veins in Saxony, Germany; the Sn-Bi-Ag veins of Uncia and Tasna, Bolivia; the polymetallic deposits of Perú; and in the NICO, IOCG deposit, Northwest Territories, Canada.

References

Fayek M. and Kyser T.K. (1995) Characteristics of auriferous and barren fluids associated with the Proterozoic Contact Lake lode gold deposit, Saskatchewan, Canada. Economic Geology, v. 90, p. 385-406.

Fuertes-Fuente M., Martin-Izard A., Nieto J.G., Maldonado C. and Varela A. (2000) Preliminary mineralogical and petrological study of the Ortosa Au-Bi-Te ore deposit: a reduced gold skarn in the northern part of the Rio Narcea Gold Belt, Asturias, Spain. Journal of Geochemical Exploration, v. 71, p. 177-190.

McQueen K.G. and Perkins C. (1995) The nature and origin of a granitoid-related gold deposit at Dargue's Reef, Major's Creek, New South Wales. Economic Geology, v. 90, p. 1646-1662.

Skirrow R.G. and Walshe J.L. (2002) Reduced and oxidized Au-Cu-Bi iron oxide deposits of the Tennant Creek Inlier, Australia: an integrated geologic and chemical model. Economic Geology, v. 97, p. 1167-1202.

Figures

bi 1 Polished surface showing silvery grey dendritic and interstitial bismuth in a siderite host, from Huttenberg, Carinthia. F.O.V. ~2.2 cm x 2.7 cm.

bi 2 Fresh surface with silvery white bismuth mineralization showing twinning, in quartz from Colorado, USA. F.O.V. ~8.7 mm x 11 mm.

bi 3 Photomicrograph of a polished thin section showing creamy white to pinkish cream bireflectance of bismuth with medium grey hematite and lighter grey loellingite (top right between the hematite and the dark grey carbonate host). Plane polarized reflected light. F.O.V. ~0.68 mm x 0.85 mm.

bi 4 Photomicrograph showing the same field of view as in **bi 3**. Twinning and light cream to pinkish brown-grey anisotropism of a slightly tarnished section are visible in cross polarized reflected light. F.O.V. ~0.68 mm x 0.85 mm.

Photographs submitted by A.H. Mumin and P.J. Adamo, Brandon University.

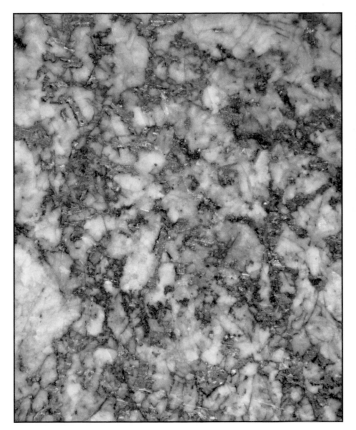

bi 1

bi 2

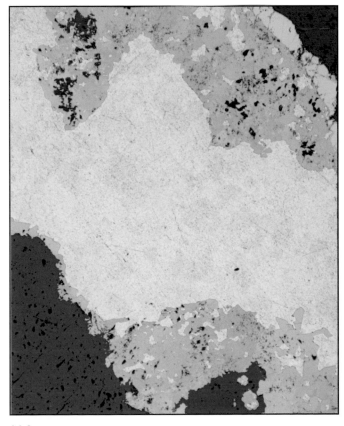

bi 3

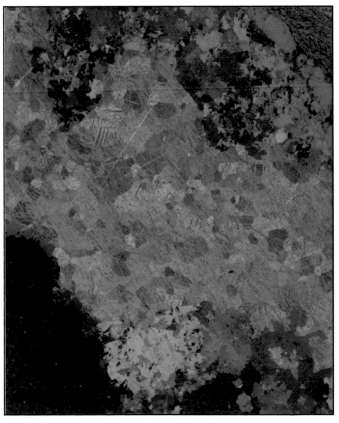

bi 4

Bismuthinite (bis)

Environment: Vein, skarn, magmatic, pegmatite

Bi_2S_3

Orthorhombic

Characteristics

Hand Specimen	
Colour	Lead grey to silvery white; grey streak
Hardness	2
Density	6.8

Polished Section			
Colour	White with slight yellow tint	Cleavage	{010} Perfect
Bireflectance	Weak to distinct	Anisotropy	Strong to very strong: greenish tints
Refl (546nm)	37.4 – 49.9	Refl (589nm)	36.79 – 48.8

Distinguishing Features

In hand specimen, bismuthinite is characterized by subhedral prismatic or acicular crystals (that may form radiating sprays), a metallic lustre (that may have a slight yellowish or bluish tint), and perfect {010} cleavage. It is very soft (thin crystals are slightly flexible) and has a high specific gravity. In polished section, it has distinct bireflectance, strong anisotropy, perfect cleavage, high reflectance (about the same or slightly higher than that of galena). The malleable character often leads to development of polysynthetic twins due to deformation.

Associated Minerals

Typically contains inclusions of native bismuth. Occurs with gold, other Bi-bearing minerals (such as josëite), Co-Ni arsenide minerals, tellurides, wolframite, cassiterite, scheelite, beryl, and various sulphides including chalcopyrite, arsenopyrite, sphalerite, and pyrite.

Mode of Occurrence

A somewhat rare sulphide mineral. Occurs as an accessory sulphide in high-temperature hydrothermal veins (e.g. Cornwall Sn-W-base-metal veins), Co-Ni arsenide veins, Bolivian Sn veins, in intrusion-related gold deposits (e.g. Pogo, Alaska), in Au, Cu, Pb-Zn, and W skarns, and in some granitic pegmatite rocks.

References

Gu X.-P., Watanabe M., Ohkawa M., Hoshino K., Shibata Y. and Chen D. (2001) Felbertalite and related bismuth sulfo-salts from the Funishan copper skarn deposit, Nanjing China. Canadian Mineralogist, v. 39, p. 1641-1652.

Springer G. (1971) The synthetic solid-solution series Bi_2S_3-BiCuPbS$_3$ (Bismuthinite-Aikinite). Neues Jahrbuch für Mineralogie, v. 1, p. 19-24.

Vanhanen E. (2001) Geology, mineralogy and geochemistry of the Fe-Co-Au-(U) deposits in the Paleoproterozoic Kuusamo Schist Belt, northeastern Finland. Geological Survey of Finland, Bulletin 399, 228 p.

Figures

bis 1 Bismuthinite in quartz gangue. Tudor Township, Hasting showing, Cobalt Ontario. Base of the coin is 1.6 cm. Specimen from I.R. Jonasson, Geological Survey of Canada. Photograph by Dan Marshall.

bis 2 Bismuthinite, Llallagua, Bolivia. Specimen number LT1257 from Lloyd Twaites. Coin diameter is 2.1 cm. Photograph by Dan Marshall.

bis 3 Bismuthinite (bis) in chalcopyrite (cp). Magnetite (mag) is replacing chalcopyrite. Guabisay, Ecuador. Teck Cominco sample R92:14275. Reflected light.

bis 4 Composite bismuthinite grain, Tudor Township, Hastings County, Ontario. Note the strong anisotropism in the two connected bismuthinite grains. The fractures parallel to cleavage are infilled by quartz. The bright yellow spots are native bismuth (bi). Plane-polarized light under crossed polars. Sample from I.R. Jonasson, Geological Survey of Canada. Photograph by Dan Marshall.

bis 1

bis 2

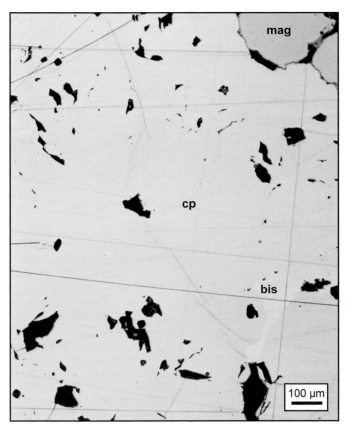

bis 3

bis 4

Bornite (bn)

Environment: Porphyry, vein, VMS, replacement

Cu_5FeS_4

Tetragonal

Characteristics

Hand Specimen	
Colour	Bronze on fresh surface, blue/purple on tarnished surface
Hardness	3
Density	4.9 – 5.4

Polished Section			
Colour	Pink-brown on fresh, rapidly tarnishing to violet or purple	Cleavage	{111} Imperfect
Bireflectance	Weak, maybe visible along grain boundaries	Anisotropy	Very weak
Refl (546nm)	21.6	Refl (589nm)	25.1

Distinguishing Features

Also known as "peacock ore", bornite is copper-bronze on a fresh surface, but tarnishes quickly to irridescent purple and blue and to a purplish black. Metallic lustre, hardness, and pale grey streak are also characteristic. In polished section, the colour is pink to orange-brown but quickly tarnishes to purple and blue. Purple tarnish and weak anisotropism are characteristic. Commonly exhibits exsolution and replacement textures with chalcopyrite, chalcocite, covellite, digenite, enargite, and tetrahedrite-tennantite.

Associated Minerals

Bornite typically occurs with other Cu-sulphides and may be associated with pyrite, sphalerite, galena, magnetite, malachite, pyrrhotite, tetrahedrite-tennantite, freibergite, and hematite.

Mode of Occurrence

Bornite is a common mineral in many copper deposits, especially in calcalkaline-alkaline porphyry deposits. It occurs more often as a hypogene and less often as a supergene mineral, and generally occurs as veinlets, disseminations, or compact granular masses. It is ubiquitous in nearly all porphyry deposits, with disseminated chalcopyrite. It also occurs in some VMS deposits (e.g. the bornite zone at Kidd Creek). In all these deposits, it is a very important ore mineral due to its high copper content. It also occurs as disseminations in basic rocks, in contact metamorphic deposits, in replacement deposits, and in pegmatite.

References

Hannington M.D., Bleeker W. and Kjarsgaard I. (1999) Sulfide mineralogy, geochemistry and ore genesis of the Kidd Creek deposit: Part 2. The bornite zone. *in* The Giant Kidd Creek Volcanogenic Massive Sulfide Deposit, Western Abitibi Subprovince, Canada, (eds.) M.D. Hannington and C.T. Barrie. Economic Geology Monograph 10, Economic Geology Publishing Company, Littleton, CO, p. 225-266.

Herzig P.M. and Hannington M.D. (2000) Polymetallic massive sulfides and gold mineralization at mid-ocean ridges and in subduction-related environments. *in* Handbook of Marine Mineral Deposits, (ed.) D.S. Cronan. p. 347-368.

Maier W.D. and Barnes S.J. (1999) The origin of Cu sulfide deposits in the Curaca Valley, Bahia, Brazil; evidence from Cu, Ni, Se, and platinum-group element concentrations. Economic Geology, v. 94, p. 165-183.

Manske S.L. and Paul A.H. (2002) Geology of a major new porphyry copper center in the Superior (Pioneer) District, Arizona. Economic Geology, v. 97, p. 197-220.

Figures

bn 1 Specimen of igneous intrusion associated breccia ore showing the weathered surface of bornite (iridescent purple and blue) intergrown with chalcopyrite (pale yellow) in a microcrystalline quartz matrix. Copper Corp. deposit, Ontario. F.O.V. 5.5 cm x 6.9 cm. Brandon University collection.

bn 2 Specimen of a fresh, polished surface of igneous intrusion associated breccia ore with bornite (coppery bronze on unweathered surfaces), chalcopyrite (pale yellow) and malachite (green) in a microcrystalline quartz matrix. Copper Corp deposit, Ontario. F.O.V. 2.8 cm x 3.5 cm. Brandon University collection.

bn 3 Photomicrograph of an Fe-oxide breccia hosted Cu-ore showing bornite (orange-beige) with lamellae and peripheral replacement by chalcopyrite (yellow). Darker blue marginal crystallites replacing bornite and chalcopyrite are covellite, pale blue is chalcocite. Sue-Dianne deposit, Northwest Territories, Canada. Plane reflected light. F.O.V. 0.45 mm x 0.56 mm. Brandon University collection.

bn 4 Photomicrograph of an Fe-oxide breccia hosted Cu-ore showing chalcopyrite (yellow) replaced sequentially by bornite (orange-beige) and covellite (shades of blue). Sue-Dianne deposit, Northwest Territories, Canada. Plane reflected light. F.O.V. 0.68 mm x 0.85 mm. Brandon University collection.

Photographs submitted by P.J. Adamo and A.H. Mumin, Brandon University.

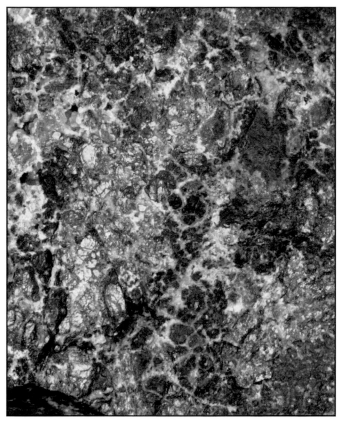

bn 1

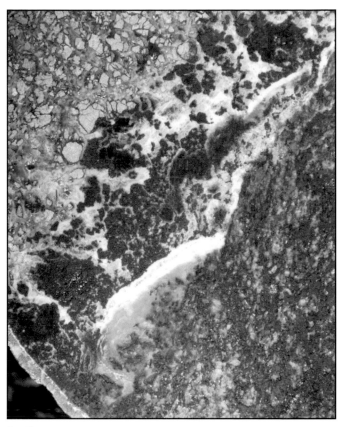

bn 2

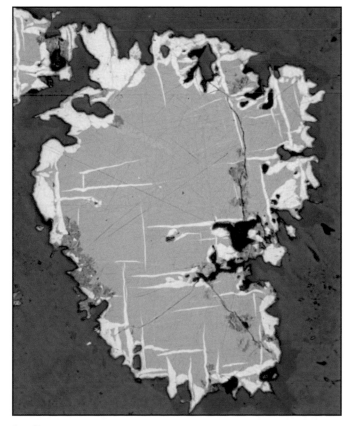

bn 3

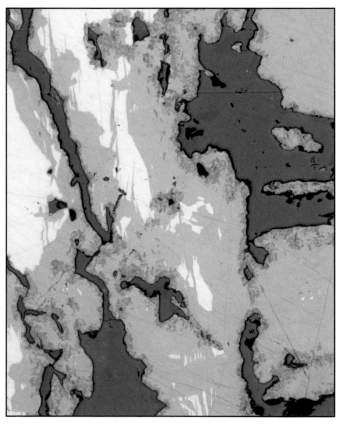

bn 4

Boulangerite (boul)

Environment: VMS, epithermal, vein, SEDEX

$Pb_5Sb_4S_{11}$

Orthorhombic

Characteristics

Hand Specimen	
Colour	Dull to metallic, bluish lead-grey to grey
Hardness	2½ – 3
Density	5.8 – 6.2

Polished Section			
Colour	White with bluish grey tint	Cleavage	{001}, {010} Imperfect
Bireflectance	Distinct, greyish-white to greenish-grey	Anisotropy	Distinct. Light to dark grey, greenish tints; rare red IR in immersion
Refl (546nm)	37.9 – 40.3	Refl (589nm)	37.2 – 39.7

Distinguishing Features

Lead grey to bluish grey colour, grey to brown streak, dull to metallic lustre, granular or fibrous crystal habit, flexibility of needle-like crystals and mineral associations are characteristic of boulangerite. In polished section, fibrous habit, well-developed cleavage parallel to fibre elongation, colour, hardness, and anisotropism are characteristic.

Associated Minerals

Galena, sphalerite, chalcopyrite, pyrite, tetrahedrite, and other Pb and Sb sulphosalts.

Mode of Occurrence

Long prismatic crystals, which may be acicular, sometimes in dense felted masses of crystals that appear hair-like, or as sparse acicular crystals that look like lint or hair disseminated among other minerals. May also form granular masses. Occurs in hydrothermal veins, stockworks, mantos, and massive sulphides. Boulangerite commonly occurs as tiny inclusions within galena.

References

Born L. and Hellne E. (1960) A structural proposal for boulangerite. American Mineralogist, v. 45, p. 1266-1271.

Hobson D.M. (1972) Boulangerite from Port Gaverne, north Cornwall. Journal of the Mineralogist Society, v. 38, p. 767-768.

Mulshaw S.C., Puig C., Spiro B. and Buchanan D.L. (1997) Genesis of epizonal Ag vein mineralization at San Bartolome in central Ecuador; textural evidence, fluid inclusions, and stable isotope geochemistry. Economic Geology, v. 92, p. 210-227.

Wagner T. and Cook N.J. (1997) Mineral reactions in sulphide systems as indicators of evolving fluid geochemistry: A case study from the Apollo Mine, Siegerland, FRG. Mineralogical Magazine, v. 61, p. 573-590.

Wagner T. and Schneider J. (2002) Lead isotope systematics of vein-type antimony mineralization, Rheinisches Schiefergebirge Germany: a case history of complex reaction and remobilization processes. Mineralium Deposita, v. 37, p 185-197.

Figures

boul 1 Boulangerite and pyrrhotite (weathered) from the Sullivan deposit, British Columbia. Specimen from Art Soregaroli. Photograph by Dan Marshall.

boul 2 Boulangerite vein from the Cleveland Pb-Zn ore-body, Stevens County, Washington. Specimen from Art Soregaroli. Photograph by Dan Marshall.

boul 3 Galena-gangue contact with laths of boulangerite (boul) in galena (gn). Teck Cominco sample R95:4037. Chachacomiri, Bolivia. Reflected light.

boul 4 Boulangerite (boul) interpenetrating into sphalerite (sph). Teck Cominco sample R95:4045. Chachacomiri, Bolivia. Reflected light.

boul 1

boul 2

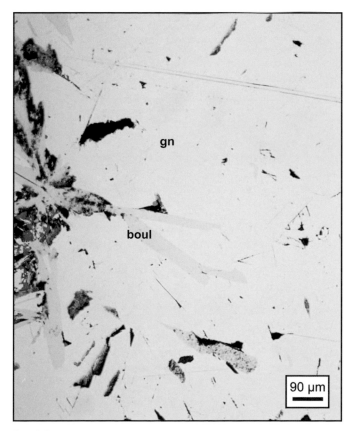

boul 3

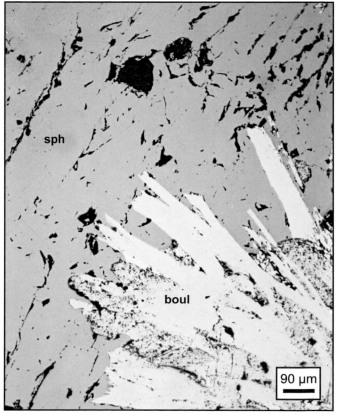

boul 4

Bournonite (bnn)

Environment: VMS, epithermal, vein, SEDEX

CuPbSbS$_3$

Orthorhombic

Characteristics

Hand Specimen	
Colour	Metallic steel-grey to black
Hardness	2½ – 3
Density	5.7 – 5.9

Polished Section			
Colour	White with a greenish shade	Cleavage	{010} Imperfect
Bireflectance	None	Anisotropy	Weak but distinctive, greenish to purplish tints
Refl (546nm)	34.4 – 36.2	Refl (589nm)	33.3 – 35.3

Distinguishing Features

Typically steel grey to black with a greyish black streak, bournonite has a metallic lustre, but may develop a dull tarnish. In polished section, bournonite takes an excellent polish, develops parallel lamellar polysynthetic twinning on {110}, and commonly occurs as inclusions in galena. The reflectance is rather high, but lower than galena.

Associated Minerals

Galena, sphalerite, chalcopyrite, pyrite, marcasite, Ag-bearing minerals, tetrahedrite-tennantite, stibnite, and other sulphosalts.

Mode of Occurrence

Twinning is common in bournonite, and repeated twinning may lead to development of multiply-twinned crystals in the form of a wheel with a jagged edge, referred to as a "cog wheel" twin. Habit is commonly tabular to short prismatic crystals, which are twinned and striated. May also occur in massive, granular aggregates. Bournonite occurs in hydrothermal veins and massive sulphide deposits.

References

Sack R.O. and Ebel D.S. (1993) As-Sb exchange energies in tetrahedrite-tennantite fahlores and bournonite-seligmannite solid solutions. Mineralogical Magazine, v. 57, p. 635-642.

Wagner T. and Cook N.J. (1997) Mineral reactions in sulphide systems as indicators of evolving fluid geochemistry; a case study from the Apollo Mine, Siegerland, FRG. Mineralogical Magazine, v. 61, p. 573-590.

Wagner T. and Jonsson E. (2001) Mineralogy of sulfosalt-rich vein-type ores, Boliden massive sulfide deposit, Skellefte District, northern Sweden. Canadian Mineralogist, v. 39, p. 855-872.

Wu I.J. and Birnie R.W. (1977) The bournonite-seligmannite solid solution. American Mineralogist, v. 62, p. 1097-1100.

Figures

bnn 1 Bournonite and quartz crystals from the Carmen deposit, Castrovirrenia District, Huancavelica Department, Perú. Specimen from Lloyd Twaites (LT988). Photograph by Dan Marshall.

bnn 2 Bournonite and quartz from the Pachapaqui deposit, Ancash Department, Perú. Coin diameter is 1.8 cm. Specimen from Art Soregaroli. Photograph by Dan Marshall.

bnn 3 Bournonite (bnn), pyrite, stibnite (stb) and sphalerite in a layered foliated siliceous gangue. Pontide, Turkey. Teck Cominco sample R92:10207. Reflected light.

bnn 4 Bournonite (bnn) and pyrargyrite (pyrg) in siliceous rock is interstitial to pyrite (py). Adjacent cement is chalcedonic silica. Teck Cominco sample R92:10208. Reflected light.

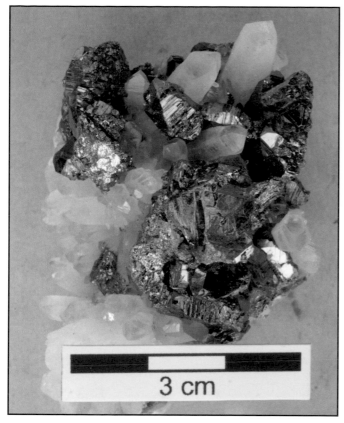

bnn 1

bnn 2

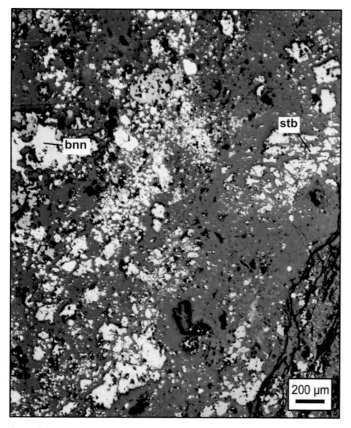

bnn 3

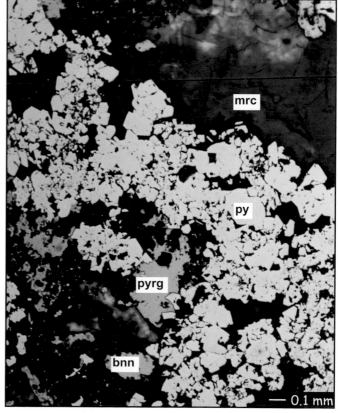

bnn 4

Cassiterite (cst)

Environment: Magmatic, pegmatitic, placer

SnO_2

Tetragonal

Characteristics

Hand Specimen	
Colour	Brown, black, yellow or grey
Hardness	6 – 7
Density	6.8 – 7.1

Polished Section			
Colour	Brownish grey	Cleavage	{100}, {110} Poor
Bireflectance	Distinct, brownish, grey	Anisotropy	Distinct, grey
Refl (546nm)	11.0 – 12.1	Refl (589nm)	10.8 – 12.0

Distinguishing Features

In hand specimen, cassiterite is typically brown to black with a white, grey, or brownish streak. Short or slender prismatic, or stubby pyramidal crystals, typically with distinctive twinning, adamantine lustre, and hardness are characteristic. In reflected light, it is grey and displays bireflectance with very low reflectance and has distinct though not very colourful anisotropism, which is commonly masked by abundant yellow to yellow-brown internal reflections. In plane polarized transmitted light, cassiterite is pleochroic, ranging from colourless to yellow to deep red and euhedral crystals are often zoned.

Associated Minerals

Associated with pyrite, arsenopyrite, molybdenite, wolframite, sphalerite, galena, rutile, hematite, magnetite, bismuth, and pyrrhotite. Cassiterite-bearing veins usually contain minerals with fluorine or boron, such as tourmaline, topaz, fluorite, and apatite. In placer deposits, cassiterite is found with other detrital heavy minerals.

Mode of Occurrence

Cassiterite is an important ore of Sn. It occurs in placers, igneous rocks, and pegmatites, but more commonly occurs in high-temperature hydrothermal veins in or near granitic rocks occurring as anhedral masses and subhedral to euhedral crystals, such as the Sn-W-Cu veins at Panasquera, Portugal. Cassiterite is also an important accessory mineral at the Kidd Creek VMS deposit and is a major constituent at Neves Corvo in Portugal. Cassiterite may sometimes result from the weathering of stannite (Cu_2FeSnS_4) and teallite ($PbSnS_2$). Wood tin is a colloform variety generally formed in veins, normally under lower temperature hydrothermal conditions.

References

Halter W.E., Williams-Jones A.E. and Kontak D.J. (1996) The role of greisenization in cassiterite precipitation at the East Kemptville tin deposit, Nova Scotia. Economic Geology, v. 91, p. 368-385.

Hennigh Q. and Hutchinson R.W. (1999) Cassiterite at Kidd Creek; An example of volcanogenic massive sulfide-hosted tin mineralization. in The Giant Kidd Creek Volcanogenic Massive Sulfide Deposit, Western Abitibi Subprovince, Canada, (eds.) M.D. Hannington and C.T. Barrie, Economic Geology Monograph 10, Economic Geology Publishing Company, Littleton, CO, p. 431-440.

Linnen R.L., Williams-Jones A.E. and Martin R.F. (1992) Evidence of magmatic cassiterite mineralization at the Nong Sua aplite-pegmatite complex. Canadian Mineralogist, v. 30, p. 739-761.

Lufkin J.F., (1977) The chemistry and mineralogy of wood-tin, Black Range, New Mexico. American Mineralogist, v. 62, p. 100-106.

Tindle A.G. and Breaks F.W. (1998) Oxide minerals of the Separation Rapids rare-element granitic pegmatite group, northwestern Ontario. Canadian Mineralogist, v. 36, p. 609-635.

Figures

cst 1 Fresh surface of tin granite from the Zaaiplaats Tinfield, Bushveld granite, South Africa. Fine black subhedral grains of cassiterite (cst) disseminated within pinky-orange altered feldspar (plagioclase and K-feldspar), quartz (colourless to white), biotite and fluorite. F.O.V. ~1.6 cm x 2.0 cm. Photograph by A.H. Mumin and P.J. Adamo, Brandon University.

cst 2 Cassiterite pebbles recovered from the Dago Hill placer gold operations in the Klondike, Yukon. A few of the pebbles show the colloform and banded textures that are characteristic of "wood tin". Tertiary rhyolites that occur in some parts of the Klondike are the likely source of the cassiterite. Photograph submitted by Dave Sinclair, Geological Survey of Canada.

cst 3 Photomicrograph of a polished thin section of the Bushveld tin granite showing an aggregate of subhedral to euhedral, colourless, pale yellow to brown cassiterite grains. Both twinning and zoning are evident. Plane polarized transmitted light, F.O.V. ~1.4 mm x 1.7 mm. Inset shows the same field of view taken in plane polarized reflected light. Photograph by A.H. Mumin and P.J. Adamo, Brandon University.

cst 4 Photomicrograph showing the same field of view as in **cst 3** in cross polarized transmitted light. Photograph by A.H. Mumin and P.J. Adamo, Brandon University.

cst 1

cst 2

cst 3

cst 4

Chalcocite (cc)

Environment: Epithermal, porphyry, veins, supergene

Cu_2S

Orthorhombic

Characteristics

Hand Specimen	
Colour	Lead-grey, darkens rapidly
Hardness	2½ – 3
Density	5.5 – 5.8

Polished Section			
Colour	White to light grey with bluish tints	Cleavage	{110} Poor
Bireflectance	Very weak, to negligible	Anisotropy	Weak but distinct when uncrossing nicols
Refl (546nm)	31.5	Refl (589nm)	30.0

Distinguishing Features

The hand-specimen colour, metallic lustre on fresh surface, shiny black to lead-grey streak, crystal habit when coarse-grained, and mineral associations are diagnostic. Fresh surfaces quickly tarnish to a dull dark grey with a bluish tint. Chalcocite plates copper onto a nail with the application of HCl. In polished section, chalcocite is usually anhedral, distinctly lamellar, and has bluish tints (distinctly visible against galena). It is very soft and may have bluish streaks due to polishing. Exsolution and replacement textures with other copper sulphides are common. Hypogene chalcocite is usually coarse grained while supergene chalcocite is fine grained and commonly appears "sooty" in polished section.

Associated Minerals

Iron and copper-iron sulphides such as pyrite, pyrrhotite, chalcopyrite, bornite, covellite, native copper, and digenite. Also associated with enargite, tetrahedrite-tennantite, sphalerite, galena, molybdenite, and stannite. It commonly appears in exsolution intergrowths with bornite or low-temperature copper sulphides and also occurs as pseudomorphs after chalcopyrite, galena, bornite, covellite, pyrite, digenite, and enargite. At surface conditions it is commonly associated with malachite, atacamite, and copper-oxides.

Mode of Occurrence

The high copper content (67% atomic ratio, almost 80% by weight) makes chalcocite an important copper ore. It is usually massive, but may form short prismatic or tabular crystals, and rarely occurs as well formed pseudohexagonal striated tabular to prismatic crystals formed by twinning. Chalcocite is hexagonal above 103°C and orthorhombic below 103°C. Chalcocite may occur as a primary mineral in veins, but its principal occurrence is as a supergene mineral in enriched zones of porphyry deposits in arid climates. Under surface conditions primary copper sulphides are oxidized. The soluble sulphates move downward reacting with the primary minerals to form chalcocite, thus enriching the ore in copper. It also occurs disseminated in basic rocks, in contact-metamorphic deposits, contact-metamorphic deposits, pegmatite, and in some red-bed copper deposits (e.g. Keweenaw Peninsula, Michigan).

References

Alyanak N. and Vogel T.A. (1974) Framboidal chalcocite from White Pine, Michigan. Economic Geology, v. 69, p. 697-703.

Kucha H., Piestrzynski A. and Wieczorek A. (1990) Cu-halloysite and fibrous chalcocite from the Zechstein copper deposits, Poland. Neues Jahrbuch für Mineralogie, v. 12, p. 553-560.

Ossandón G., Fréraut R., Gustafson L.B., Lindsay D.D. and Zentilli M. (2001) Geology of the Chuquicamata mine: A progress report. Economic Geology, v. 96, p. 249-270.

Sillitoe R.H., Jaramillo L. and Castro H. (1984) Geologic exploration of a molybdenum-rich porphyry copper deposit at Mocoa, Colombia. Economic Geology, v. 79, p. 106-123.

Figures

cc 1 Fresh and oxidized chalcocite with minor pyrite and quartz, Leonard deposit, Butte, Montana. Coin diameter is 1.9 cm. Specimen (S62.30) from Art Soregaroli. Photograph by Dan Marshall.

cc 2 Sooty chalcocite coatings on pyrite from Butte, Montana. Specimen (S58.92) from Art Soregaroli. Photograph by Dan Marshall.

cc 3 Chalcocite (cc) replacing pyrite. The chalcocite ranges in colour from grey to blue. Quebrada Blanca deposit, Chile. Teck Cominco specimen R96:414.

cc 4 Pyrite (py) replaced by chalcocite (cc) which in turn is replaced by hematite and covellite (cv). Gangue is quartz. Teck Cominco specimen R93:4396. Mamainse, Ontario.

cc 1

cc 2

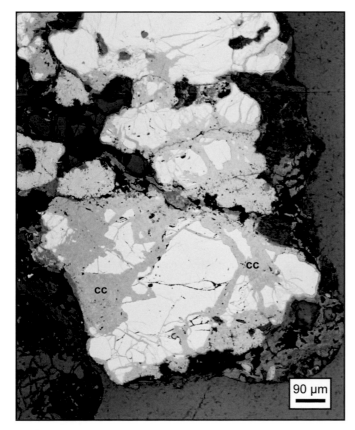

cc 3

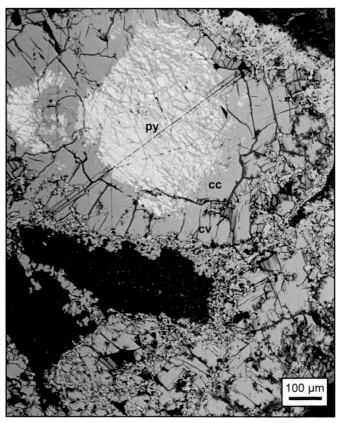

cc 4

Chalcopyrite (cp)

Environment: Porphyry, VMS, Magmatic, SEDEX, epithermal, vein, skarn

$CuFeS_2$

Tetragonal

Characteristics

Hand Specimen	
Colour	Brass yellow
Hardness	3½ – 4½
Density	4.1 – 4.3

Polished Section			
Colour	Yellow to brassy yellow	Cleavage	{011}, {111} Poor
Bireflectance	Weak	Anisotropy	Weak, rarely distinct, grey-blue to yellow-green
Refl (546nm)	35.7 – 36.9	Refl (589nm)	38.7 – 39.8

Distinguishing Features

The brassy yellow colour and iridescent bluish to purplish to greenish tarnish on weathered surfaces distinguish it from pyrite and pyrrhotite. The colour may resemble native gold, but chalcopyrite is much harder, with a brittle conchoidal fracture, lower density, and dark greenish black streak. It can be distinguished from pyrite by its hardness. In polished section, chalcopyrite is brass yellow, with rather high reflectance, and weak anisotropism. Distinct grey-blue to yellow-green polarization colours show well under slightly uncrossed nicols. Twinning is common and chalcopyrite is usually anhedral. It is regularly observed in exsolution intergrowths with other copper sulphides and pyrrhotite, and occurs in sphalerite as chalcopyrite disease.

Associated Minerals

Chalcopyrite occurs with pyrite, molybdenite, pyrrhotite, pentlandite, bornite, digenite, magnetite, and many other minerals. It often alters along cracks and grain boundaries to covellite, chalcocite, and malachite. Intergrowths occur with tetrahedrite, cubanite, galena, and sphalerite.

Mode of Occurrence

Chalcopyrite is the most common copper mineral and is found in almost all sulphide deposits. Chalcopyrite can be massive, crystalline disseminated, and/or intergrown. It occurs as medium- to coarse-grained anhedral aggregates and rarely as well developed tetrahedral crystals. It forms in almost all ore forming environments. Disseminated chalcopyrite is the most important ore mineral in hypogene porphyry deposits, and is a major constituent of VMS and Cu-skarn deposits.

References

Barton P.B. Jr. and Bethke P.M. (1987) Chalcopyrite disease in sphalerite; pathology and epidemiology. American Mineralogist, v. 72, p. 451-467.

Bortnikov N.S., Genkin A.D., Dobrovol M.G., Muravitskaya G.N. and Filimonova A.A. (1991) The nature of chalcopyrite inclusions in sphalerite; exsolution, coprecipitation, or "disease"?. Economic Geology, v. 86, p. 1070-1082.

Kumarapeli P.S., Kheang L., Höy L. and Pintson H. (1999) Chalcopyrite-bornite and chalcopyrite-bornite-barite in the Acton Vale Limestone, southeastern Quebec; mineralized shelf-margin slivers in a Taconian nappe. Canadian Journal of Earth Sciences, v. 27, p. 27-39.

Mizuta T. and Scott S.D. (1997) Kinetics of iron depletion near pyrrhotite and chalcopyrite inclusions in sphalerite; the sphalerite speedometer. Economic Geology, v. 92, p. 772-783.

Figures

cp 1 Brassy to yellow chalcopyrite in a siliceous matrix. Coin diameter is 2.1 cm. Simon Fraser University collection. Photograph by Holly Keyes, Ashton Mining.

cp 2 Chalcopyrite veinlets and disseminations in garnetiferous calc-silicate gangue. Oro Denoro deposit, British Columbia. Specimen S75.8.19 from Art Soregaroli. Photograph by Dan Marshall.

cp 3 Irregular twinned chalcopyrite (cp) with pyrite (py) and pyrrhotite (po). Blue Lake, Quebec. F.O.V. 4 mm. Submitted by Georges Beaudoin, Université Laval.

cp 4 Massive chalcopyrite (cp) replaces pyrite (py) crystals and is mutually intergrown with sphalerite (sph). Plane polarized reflected light. Teck Cominco Specimen R97:11136.

cp 1

cp 2

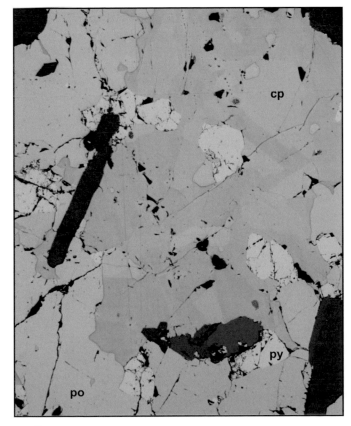

cp 3

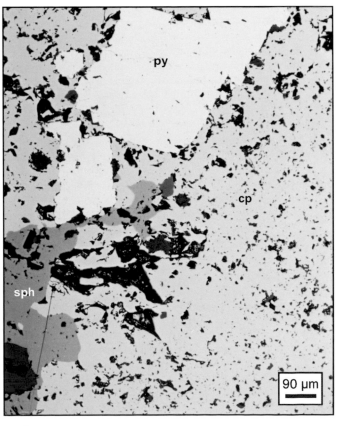

cp 4

Chromite (chr)

Environment: Magmatic

$(Fe,Mg)(Cr,Al)_2O_4$

Cubic

Characteristics

Hand Specimen	
Colour	Iron black to brownish black
Hardness	5½
Density	4.6

Polished Section			
Colour	Dark grey to brownish grey	Cleavage	None
Bireflectance	Absent	Anisotropy	Very weak, usually absent
Refl (546nm)	12.0	Refl (589nm)	11.7

Distinguishing Features

In hand specimen, the dark brown to black colour, greasy sub-metallic lustre, brown streak, massive or granular (and rarely octahedral crystal) habit, and association with ultramafic minerals are characteristic. Chromite is also weakly magnetic. In polished section, the dark grey to brownish grey (darker than magnetite) colour, and low reflectance are characteristic for chromite. Internal reflections are brown-red in Mg- and Al-rich specimens, but absent in Fe-rich specimens. Chromite can occur as myrmekitic intergrowths with surrounding gangue minerals. Usually seen as rounded, euhedral grains in silicate matrix. It takes a good polish and is isotropic, but anomalous anisotropism is sometimes observed in Zn-rich and deformed varieties.

Associated Minerals

Associated with magnetite, ilmenite, pentlandite, pyrrhotite, hematite, and PGMs. It is also associated with olivine, pyroxene, anorthite, and serpentine.

Mode of Occurrence

Chromite is a principal ore of chromium. Chromite is a common constituent of peridotites and other ultrabasic rocks and of serpentinites derived from them. Large chromite ore deposits are thought to have been derived by cumulate magmatic differentiation. Important deposits such as the Bushveld igneous complex of South Africa and the Great Dyke of Zimbabwe contain numerous seams of chromite enclosed in pyroxenite (stratiform deposits). Due to its resistance to erosion, chromite may accumulate in laterite and placer deposits. Chromite also occurs in meteorites.

References

Roach T.S., Roeder P.L.. and Hulbert L.J. (1998) Composition of chromite in the upper chromite, Muskox layered intrusion, Northwest Territories. Canadian Mineralogist, v. 36, p. 117-135.

Rubin A.E. (2003) Chromite-plagioclase assemblages as a new shock indicator; implications for the shock and thermal histories of ordinary chondrites. Geochimica et Cosmochimica Acta, v. 67, p. 2695-2709.

Stowe C.W. (1994) Compositions and tectonic settings of chromite deposits through time. Economic Geology, v. 89, p. 528-546.

Tesalina S.G., Nimis P., Auge T., et al. (2003) Origin of chromite in mafic-ultramafic-hosted hydrothermal massive sulfides from the Main Uralian Fault, South Urals, Russia. Lithos, v. 70, p. 39-59.

Zingg A.J. (1996) Recrystallization and the origin of layering in the Bushveld Complex. Lithos, v. 37, p. 15-37.

Figures

chr 1   Charcoal grey cumulate chromite laminations in norite from the Critical zone (base of Merensky reef), Bushveld complex, South Africa. F.O.V. ~3.7 cm x 4.6 cm.

chr 2   Black granular aggregate of chromite from the main chromite seam of the Basal zone, Potgietersrust, Transvaal, Bushveld complex, South Africa. F.O.V. ~3.7 cm x 4.6 cm.

chr 3   Photomicrograph of subhedral to rounded lighter grey chromite (chr) from the Rusterberg Platinum Mine, Zimbabwe. Chalcopyrite, pyrrhotite and pentlandite appear anomalously bright due to grey silicate background. Chromite appears darker grey compared to **chr 4**. This results from decreased light intensity to retain the colour in the sulphides. Polished thin section, plane polarized reflected light. F.O.V. ~1.4 mm x 1.7 mm.

chr 4   Photomicrograph of subhedral to rounded lighter grey cumulate chromite(chr) from the Critical zone of Merensky reef, Bushveld complex, South Africa. Polished thin section, plane polarized reflected light. F.O.V. ~1.4 mm x 1.7 mm.

Photographs submitted by P.J. Adamo and A.H. Mumin, Brandon University.

chr 1

chr 2

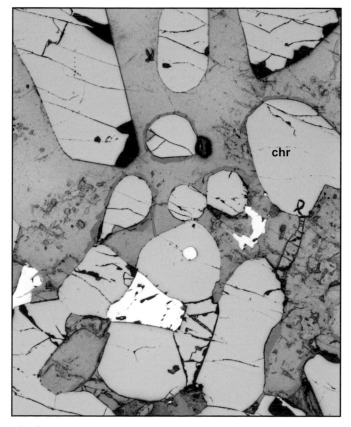

chr 3

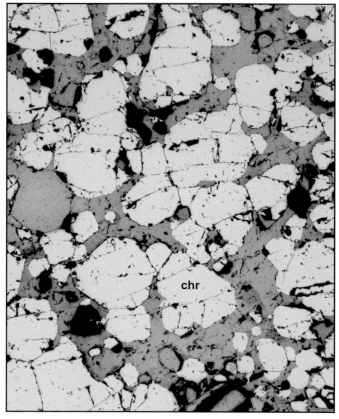

chr 4

Chrysocolla (chry)

Environment: Secondary, supergene, porphyry

$(CuAl)_2H_2Si_2O_5 \cdot nH_2O$

Orthorhombic

Characteristics

Hand Specimen	
Colour	Green, greenish blue
Hardness	2 – 4
Density	2.0 – 2.4

Polished Section			
Colour	Dark grey	Cleavage	Absent
Bireflectance	Absent to weak	Anisotropy	Absent to strong
Refl (546nm)	Very low	Refl (589nm)	Very low

Distinguishing Features

Chrysocolla has a distinct pale blue to blue-green colour, white streak, conchoidal fracture and a vitreous to earthy lustre. It has a low density and hardness and is commonly botryoidal in habit. Chrysocolla can range from translucent to opaque; therefore, it has optical properties under both reflected and transmitted light. Under plane transmitted light, chrysocolla appears translucent to yellow-cream coloured. Under crossed nicols, it has a high birefringence, displaying high third-order colours. In reflected light, it has a very low bireflectance, which yields a dark grey colour. In hand specimen, chrysocolla adheres to a moistened finger and colours a flame green.

Associated Minerals

Commonly occurs with copper-bearing minerals such as cuprite, azurite, malachite, and native copper derived from copper-bearing sulphide minerals.

Mode of Occurrence

An alteration product of copper minerals, it is commonly mixed with other secondary copper minerals and hydrated copper silicates in the upper levels of vein and supergene altered porphyry deposits. It occurs as opaque to translucent crusts or seam fillings in shades of blue, green, brown, and black with inclusions.

References

Bouzari F. and Clark A.H. (2002) Anatomy, evolution, and metallogenic significance of the supergene orebody of the Cerro Colorado porphyry copper deposit, I region, northern Chile. Economic Geology, v. 97, p. 1701-1740.

Cuadra P. and Rojas G. (2001) Oxide mineralization at the Radomiro Tomic porphyry copper deposit, northern Chile. Economic Geoogy, v. 96, p. 387-400.

Kelm U., Sanhueza V., Madejova J., Sucha V. and Elsass F. (2001) Evaluation of identification methods for chrysocolla - A Cu-smectite-like hydrous silicate: Implications for heap-leaching extraction of copper. Geologica Carpathica, v. 52, p. 111-121.

Trista D. and Kojima S. (2003) Mineral paragenesis and fluid inclusions of some pluton-hosted vein-type copper deposits in the Coastal Cordillera, northern Chile. Resource Geology, v. 53, p. 21-28.

Figures

chry 1 Chrysocolla (green and blue) and Fe-oxide-cemented weathered capping over Cu mineralization from Miami Arizona. F.O.V. ~4.8 cm x 6.0 cm.

chry 2 Chrysocolla (green and blue) veins cementing quartz stockwork breccia from Twin Buttes, Arizona. Cut wet face. F.O.V. ~6.2 cm x 7.8 cm.

chry 3 Photomicrograph of pale greenish yellow chrysocolla showing an intra-vein radial growth pattern. Polished thin section, plane polarized transmitted light. F.O.V. ~0.34 mm x 0.43 mm.

chry 4 Photomicrograph showing the same field of view as in **chry 3**, and taken in cross polarized transmitted light. Polished thin section. F.O.V. ~0.34 mm x 0.43 mm.

Photographs submitted by A.H. Mumin and P.J. Adamo, Brandon University.

chry 1

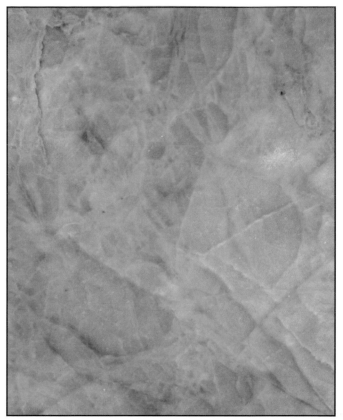

chry 2

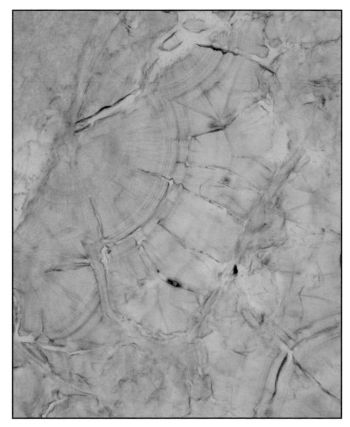

chry 3

chry 4

Cinnabar (ci)

Environment: Epithermal, magmatic, vein, hot spring

HgS

Trigonal

Characteristics

Hand Specimen	
Colour	Vermillion-red when pure to brownish red when impure
Hardness	2½
Density	8.0 – 8.2

Polished Section			
Colour	White with bluish grey to reddish tint	Cleavage	{1010} Perfect
Bireflectance	Weak to distrinct	Anisotropy	Grey-blue-green; strong, but masked by internal reflection
Refl (546nm)	28.2 – 29.1	Refl (589nm)	27.6 – 28.4

Distinguishing Features

Cinnabar is distinguished in hand specimen by its brownish red to scarlet colour, scarlet streak, softness, and high density. Usually occurs as anhedral crystals, but also forms euhedral single crystals and polycrystalline aggregates. In polished section, cinnabar is white with grayish tints, reflectance is moderate, anisotropism is strong but masked by extensive red internal reflections.

Associated Minerals

Commonly associated with pyrite, marcasite, stibnite, realgar, native gold, orpiment, galena, enargite, and sulphides of copper and opal, chalcedony, quartz, barite, calcite, or fluorite.

Mode of Occurrence

Cinnabar is the only common mineral of mercury and constitutes the most important ore mineral of mercury. Cinnabar occurs in the Almaden district in Spain and Tongren, Guizhou Province and other locations in China. It has also been mined from deposits in California and British Columbia. It occurs as vein fillings and disseminations near volcanic rocks and hot springs, deposited near surface from alkaline solutions. Usually occurs as encrustations and disseminations through the rock. Cinnabar is a common mineral in epithermal gold deposits, and is found at Hemlo, Ontario. Mercury was an essential component throughout history for the recovery of gold by amalgamation, and is an important pathfinder element for epithermal deposits.

References

Gray J.E., Crock J.G. and Fey D.L. (2002) Environmental geochemistry of abandoned mercury mines in West-Central Nevada, USA. Applied Geochemistry, v. 17, p. 1069-1079.

McPherson R. (1999) Two great California cinnabar mines; on the trail to fabled quicksilver. Rock and Gem, v. 29, p. 48-50, 78.

Prol-Ledesma R.M., Canet C., Melgarejo J.C., Tolson G., Rubio-Ramos M.A., Cruz-Ocampo J.C., Ortega-Osorio A., Torres-Vera M.A. and Reyes A. (2002) Cinnabar deposition in submarine coastal hydrothermal vents, pacific margin of central Mexico. Economic Geology, v. 97, p. 1331-1340.

Wallace A.R. (2003) Geology of the Ivanhoe Hg-Au district, northern Nevada: Influence of Miocene volcanism, lakes, and active faulting on epithermal mineralization. Economic Geology, v. 98, p. 409-424.

Zhang X-C., Spiro B., Halls C., Stanley C.J. and Yang K-Y. (2003) Sediment-hosted disseminated gold deposits in Southwest Guizhou, PRC; their geological setting and origin in relation to mineralogical, fluid inclusion, and stable-isotope characteristics. International Geology Review, v. 45, p. 407-470.

Figures

ci 1 Fresh surface of mercury ore from Almaden, Spain. Reddish veins and disseminations of cinnabar are dispersed through a siliceous host rock. F.O.V. ~2.6 cm x 3.3 cm.

ci 2 Red cinnabar veining in a siliceous host rock from Almaden, Spain. F.O.V. ~2.9 cm x 3.6 cm.

ci 3 Photomicrograph of light grey weakly bireflectant cinnabar with reddish tinges due to abundant internal reflections. Specimen is from Almaden, Spain. Polished thin section in plane polarized reflected light. F.O.V. ~0.68 mm x 0.85 mm.

ci 4 Photomicrograph showing brownish red to brilliant red internal reflections of cinnabar masking strong anisotropism. Field of view is the same as in **ci 3**, taken in cross polarized reflected light. F.O.V. ~0.68 mm x 0.85 mm.

Photographs submitted by A.H. Mumin and P.J. Adamo, Brandon University.

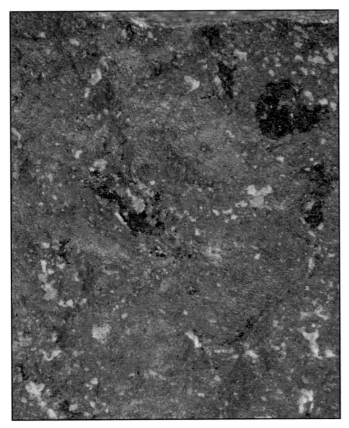

ci 1

ci 2

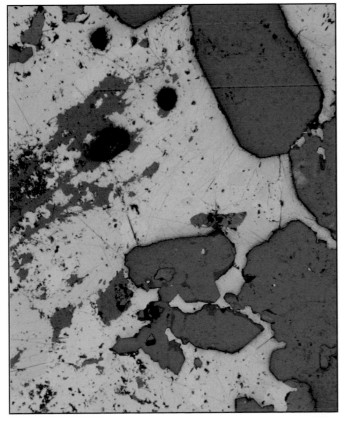

ci 3

ci 4

Cobaltite (cob)

Environment: Vein, magmatic, epithermal

CoAsS

Pseudocubic / Orthorhombic

Characteristics

Hand Specimen	
Colour	Silver-white, pinkish tint
Hardness	5½
Density	5.9 – 6.3

Polished Section			
Colour	White with pink or violet tint	Cleavage	Pseudocubic, perfect on {100}
Bireflectance	Weak, pink to whitish	Anisotropy	Weak to distinct in oil, blue, brown
Refl (546nm)	50.5	Refl (589nm)	52.7

Distinguishing Features

On a fresh surface cobaltite is white to silver-grey with metallic lustre and dark grey streak. It is usually massive in habit, however if crystalline it may display perfect cleavage in three directions. Its density is slightly higher than average for metallic minerals. Weathered cobaltite commonly has a slight pinkish tinge due to the presence of erythrite (known as cobalt bloom: $Co_3[AsO_4]^2 \cdot 8[H_2O]$). In polished section, cobaltite is white with a pinkish tint and high reflectance. Its weak anisotropism distinguishes it from nickeline, which is strongly anisotropic.

Associated Minerals

Occurs with erythrite, native silver, arsenopyrite, native bismuth, Ni-Co arsenides, skutterudite and other Co-bearing minerals, nickeline, chalcopyrite, and uraninite.

Mode of Occurrence

Commonly occurs as polycrystalline aggregates and as euhedral crystals. Twinning, zoning, and cleavage may be visible. Cobaltite typically occurs in high-temperature deposits, as disseminations and grains in metamorphosed rocks, or in vein deposits with other cobalt and nickel minerals. A notable occurrence of cobaltite is at Cobalt, Ontario.

References

Barkov A.Y., Thibault Y., Laajoki K.V.O., Melezhik V.A. and Nilsson A.P. (1999) Zoning and substitutions in Co-Ni-(Fe)-PGE sulfarsenides from the Mount General'skaya layered intrusion, Arctic Russia. Canadian Mineralogist, v. 37, p. 127-142.

Fleet M.E. and Burns P.C. (1990) Structure and twinning of cobaltite. Canadian Mineralogist, v. 28, p. 719-723.

Moreton S. (1996) The Alva silver mine; Silver Glen, Alva, Scotland. Mineralogical Record, v. 27, p. 405-414.

Petruk W., Harris D.C. and Stewart J.M. (1971) Characteristics of the arsenides, sulpharsenides, and antimonides. Canadian Mineralogist, v. 11, p. 150-186.

Wagner T. and Lorenz J. (2002) Mineralogy of complex Co-Ni-Bi vein mineralization, Bieber Deposit, Spessart, Germany. Mineralogical Magazine, v. 66, p. 385-407.

Figures

cob 1 Cobaltite (pseudo octahedra) with calcite and magnetite, Merry Widow Mine, Vancouver Island, British Columbia. Lloyd Twaites collection, specimen LT822. Photograph by Dan Marshall.

cob 2 Cobaltite (grey)-erythrite (pink) with carbonate gangue. Simon Fraser University collection. Photograph by Dan Marshall.

cob 3 Cobaltite (cob), skutterudite (sk), safflorite (saf) and nickeline (nic) in plane polarized light. Specimen from Ed van Hees, Wayne State University. Photograph by Dan Marshall.

cob 4 Corresponding photo taken in partly crossed polarized light. Note the blue and brown anisotropic colours for safflorite, the strong anisotropic pink colour for nickeline, and the slight anisotropism in cobaltite.

cob 1

cob 2

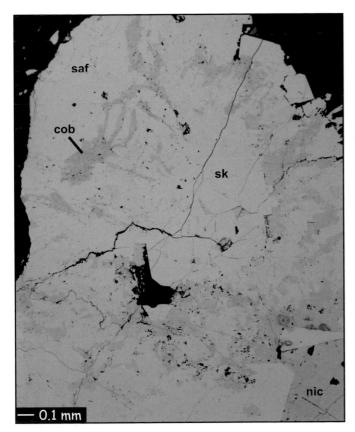

cob 3

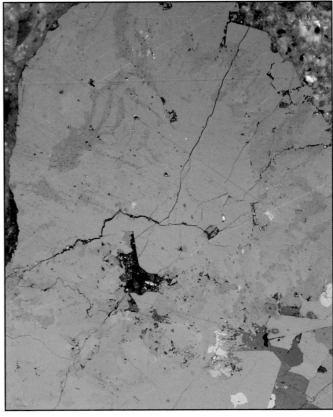

cob 4

Copper (cu)

Environment: Porphyry, secondary, supergene, magmatic

Cu   Cubic

Characteristics

Hand Specimen	
Colour	Copper-red, brown-red tarnish
Hardness	2½ – 3
Density	8.9

Polished Section			
Colour	Deep pink, tarnishes brown	Cleavage	Absent
Bireflectance	Weak	Anisotropy	Isotropic
Refl (546nm)	47.5	Refl (589nm)	65.9

Distinguishing Features

In hand specimen, the colour on fresh and tarnished surfaces, copper-red streak, hackly fracture, high specific gravity, and malleability are characteristic for native copper. In polished section, copper is very reflective. It has a distinctly reddish colour, takes a poor polish with frequent scratches. Although copper is isotropic, the scratches may appear anisotropic.

Associated Minerals

Small amounts of native copper occur associated with cuprite, malachite, and azurite at many localities in the oxidized supergene zones of primary copper deposits. It also occurs with chalcocite, enargite, bornite, pyrrhotite, iron, and magnetite. In basalt-hosted deposits, native copper may be found associated with chalcocite, bornite, chalcopyrite, and pyrite.

Mode of Occurrence

Occurs as coarse- to fine-grained aggregates, rarely as dendritic or spear-like crystals, wires, or very rarely as individual crystals (cubes and octahedrons). Most primary deposits of native copper are associated with subaerial flood-basalt lavas, where deposition of copper resulted from the diagenetic reactions of copper-bearing brine solutions within the basaltic host rocks. The most important locality for native copper is the Keweenaw Peninsula, Michigan, on the southern shore of Lake Superior (USA). In these deposits, the native copper fills amygdules and fractures within basalt and also occurs as cement in conglomerate. As noted above, native copper also occurs in the supergene oxidized zones of primary copper deposits. In Canada, the Afton alkaline porphyry deposit in British Columbia contained considerable native copper, but the genesis (hypogene versus supergene) is uncertain.

References

Brown A.C. (1971) Zoning in the White Pine copper deposit, Ontonagon County, Michigan. Economic Geology, v. 66, p. 543-573.

Chamberlain J.A., McLeod C.R., Traill R.J. and Lachance G.R. (1965) Native metals in the Muskox intrusion. Canadian Journal of Earth Sciences, v. 2, p. 188-215.

Kirkham R.V. (1996) Volcanic Redbed Copper. in Geology of Canadian Mineral Deposit Types, (ed.) O.R. Eckstrand, W.D. Sinclair, and R.I. Thorpe. Geological Survey of Canada, Geology of Canada No. 8, p. 241-252.

Subías I., Fanlo I., Mateo E. and García-Veigas J. (2003) A model for the diagenetic formation of sandstone-hosted copper deposits in Tertiary sedimentary rocks, Aragón (NE Spain): S/C ratios and sulphur isotope systematics. Ore Geology Reviews, v. 23, p. 55-70.

Figures

cu 1   Black and green (oxidized) copper with hackly fracture. Keweenaw, Michigan. Specimen S03.200 from Art Soregaroli. Photography by Dan Marshall. Scale bar in centimetres.

cu 2   Native copper detail, showing dendritic texture (60 second acid wash to remove surface oxidation). Arizona. F.O.V. ~1.0 cm x 1.2 cm. Submitted by P.J. Adamo and A.H. Mumin, Brandon University.

cu 3   Native copper. Edge of coin is 2 cm. Simon Fraser University collection. Photograph by Holly Keyes.

cu 4   Photomicrograph of a polished slab of native copper showing the pinky orange colour of a clean unoxidized surface, taken in plane polarized reflected light. F.O.V. ~1.4 mm x 1.7 mm. Submitted by P.J. Adamo and A.H. Mumin, Brandon University.

cu 1

cu 2

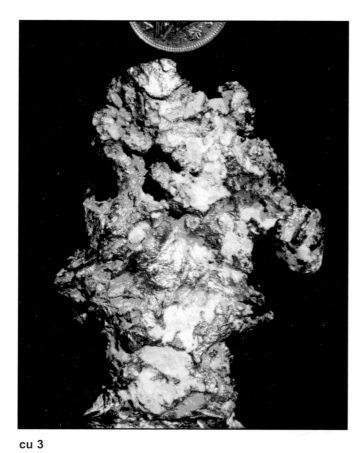

cu 3

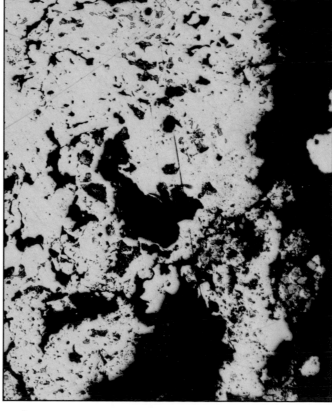

cu 4

Covellite (cv)

Environment: Porphyry, vein, secondary, IOCG

CuS

Hexagonal

Characteristics

Hand Specimen	
Colour	Indigo blue or darker
Hardness	1½ – 2
Density	4.6 – 4.8

Polished Section			
Colour	Indigo blue with violet tint to bluish white in air	Cleavage	{0001} Perfect, giving flexible plates
Bireflectance	Strong blue-violet to bluish white	Anisotropy	Extreme, red-orange to brownish
Refl (546nm)	6.3 – 21.4	Refl (589nm)	3.3 – 19.1

Distinguishing Features

Covellite has a characteristic deep indigo-blue colour often with a purple iridescence. It has a dark grey to black streak, a micaceous cleavage, and is very soft. It is usually massive in habit or occurs as disseminated grains in sulphide ore deposits, but may form thin platy hexagonal crystals. In polished section, its strong blue-violet to bluish white bireflectance and orange to reddish brown anisotropism are unmistakable. Some aggregate specimens exhibit deformation and recrystallization structures.

Associated Minerals

Commonly seen in association with copper and iron sulphides such as pyrite, chalcopyrite, chalcocite, digenite, and bornite, and is derived from them by alteration. Occurs also with enargite, sphalerite, native copper, cuprite, hematite, limonite, goethite, linnaeite, luzonite, and tetrahedrite-tennantite.

Mode of Occurrence

Covellite is not an abundant mineral but is found in many copper deposits as a product of supergene enrichment. It generally occurs as platy to compact masses and micaceous plates, disseminated, in veinlets, and commonly as partial replacements of other copper minerals. Covellite is a common supergene mineral associated with porphyry copper deposits (e.g. Butte, Montana) and IOCG deposits. It also occurs with chalcocite in red-bed copper deposits.

References

Gablina I.F., Mozgova N.N., Borodaev Y.S., Stepanova T.V., Cherkashev G.A. and Il'in M.I. (2000) Copper sulfide associations in recent oceanic ores of the Logachev hydrothermal field (Mid-Atlantic Ridge, 14° 45' N). Geology Ore Deposits, v. 42, p. 296-316.

Landtwing M.R., Dillenbeck E.D., Leake M.H. and Heinrich C.A. (2002) Evolution of the breccia-hosted porphyry Cu-Mo-Au deposit at Agua Rica, Argentina: Progressive unroofing of a magmatic hydrothermal system. Economic Geology, v. 97, p. 1273-1292.

Large D.J., MacQuaker J., Vaughan D.J., Sawlowicz Z. and Gize A.P. (1995) Evidence for low-temperature alteration of sulfides in the Kupferschiefer copper deposits of southwestern Poland. Economic Geology, v. 90, p. 2143-2155.

Moss R. and Scott S.D. (1996) Silver in sulfide chimneys and mounds from 13° N and 21° N, East Pacific Rise. Canadian Mineralogist, v. 34, p. 697-716.

Ossandón G., Fréraut R., Gustafson L.B., Lindsay D.D. and Zentilli M. (2001) Geology of the Chuquicamata mine: A progress report. Economic Geology, v. 96, p. 249-270.

Figures

cv 1 Specimen of porphyry associated vein ore with covellite veins (blue) and disseminated grains and veinlets of pyrite (pale yellow) within altered porphyry. Butte, Montana. F.O.V. 5.8 cm x 7.3 cm. Brandon University collection.

cv 2 Specimen of porphyry associated massive vein ore with indigo blue covellite and disseminated grains and veinlets of pyrite (pale yellow). Butte, Montana. F.O.V. 6.4 cm x 8.0 cm. Brandon University collection.

cv 3 Photomicrograph of a hydrothermal Fe-oxide-breccia hosted copper ore showing light to dark blue bireflectance of covellite with remnants of orange-beige bornite. Parallel fractures result from volume loss during alteration of bornite. Sue-Dianne deposit, Northwest Territories, Canada. Plane reflected light. F.O.V. 0.14 mm x 0.17 mm.

cv 4 Photomicrograph same view as **cv 3** showing strong anisotropism of covellite from pinky beige to bright orange and reddish brown. Sue-Dianne deposit, Northwest Territories, Canada. Reflected light with crossed polarizers. F.O.V. 0.14 mm x 0.17 mm.

Photographs submitted by P.J. Adamo and A.H. Mumin, Brandon University.

cv 1

cv 2

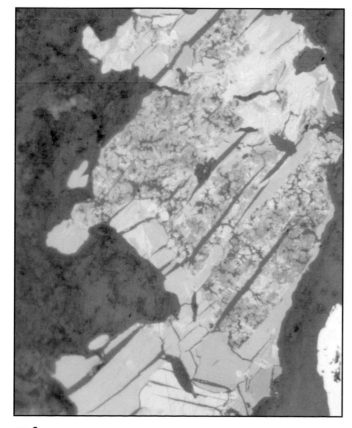

cv 3

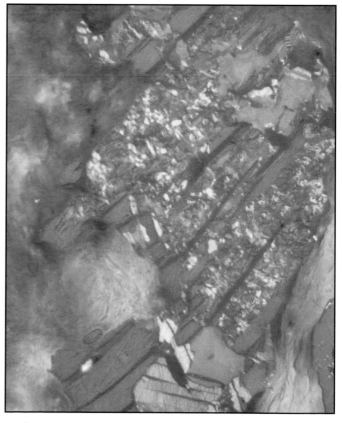

cv 4

Cubanite (cub)

Environment: Epithermal, vein, magmatic

$CuFe_2S_3$

Orthorhombic

Characteristics

Hand Specimen	
Colour	Metallic brass/ bronze yellow
Hardness	3½
Density	4.0 – 4.2

Polished Section			
Colour	Creamy grey to yellowish brown	Cleavage	Poor
Bireflectance	Distinct, greyish to brownish	Anisotropy	Strong, brownish to blue
Refl (546nm)	36.6 – 41.2	Refl (589nm)	38.5 – 42.2

Distinguishing Features

In hand specimen, the colour resembles chalcopyrite. Cubanite is strongly magnetic, often displaying good crystal habit of elongated or thick tabular crystals. Twinning is common with longitudinal striations on most crystal faces. Cubanite has conchoidal fracture, no cleavage, and has a black streak. In polished section, the bireflectance and strong anisotropism, good polish, and rather high reflectance are characteristic.

Associated Minerals

Chalcopyrite (commonly as exsolution lamellae or coarse laths in chalcopyrite), pyrrhotite, sphalerite, galena, magnetite, pentlandite, and arsenopyrite. Isocubanite is a high-temperature polymorph of cubanite.

Mode of Occurrence

A relatively rare ore mineral of copper, it rarely occurs well crystallized. Mostly occurs as isolated grains, granular aggregates, or coarse lamellae and inclusions in chalcopyrite. Complexly twinned well-developed crystal specimens do occur in the Henderson No. 2 mine in the Chibougamau (see photos) and the Thompson mine in Manitoba. In the deep copper zones of the Sudbury Cu-Ni magmatic sulphide ores, it is an important ore mineral with chalcopyrite. Isocubanite is reported from deep-sea hydrothermal vent sulphides.

References

Cabri L.J., Hall R.S., Szymanski J.T. and Stewart J.M. (1973) On the transformation of cubanite. Canadian Mineralogist, v. 12, p. 33-38.

Caye R., Cervelle B., Cesbron F., Oudin E., Picot P. and Pillard F. (1988). Isocubanite, a new definition of the cubic polymorph of cubanite $CuFe_2S_3$. Mineralogical Magazine, v. 52, p. 509-14.

Leveques A. (1983) Cubanite from Chibougamau Quebec. Mineralogical Record, v. 14, p. 151-155.

Naldrett A.J., Singh J., Krstic S. and Li C. (2000) The mineralogy of the Voisey's Bay Ni-Cu-Co deposit, northern Labrador, Canada: Influence of oxidation state on textures and mineral compositions. Economic Geology, v. 95, p. 889-900.

Pruseth K.L., Mishra B. and Bernhardt H.J. (1999) An experimental study on cubanite irreversibility: Implications for natural chalcopyrite-cubanite intergrowths. European Journal of Mineralogy, v. 11, p. 471-476.

Szymanski J.T. (1974) A refinement of the structure of cubanite, $CuFe_2S_3$. Zeitschrift für Kristallographie, v. 140, p. 218-239.

Figures

cub 1 Cubanite, Henderson #2 Mine, Chibougamau, Quebec. Scale bar is 5 cm long. Specimen (S91.41) from Art Soregaroli. Photography by Dan Marshall.

cub 2 Cubanite crystals on calcite. Henderson 2 Mine, Quebec. F.O.V. 5 cm. Submitted by Musée de géologie René-Bureau. Photograph by Georges Beaudoin, Université Laval.

cub 3 Cubanite (cub), chalcopyrite (cp) and pentlandite (pn) encircled by a large pyrite (py) grain. Mesaba deposit, Minnesota. Teck Cominco specimen RO1:3998. Plane polarized reflected light.

cub 4 Cubanite exsolution (cub) in chalcopyrite (cp) in contact with pyrrhotite (po). Blue Lake, Quebec. F.O.V. 7 mm, plane polarized reflected light. Submitted by Georges Beaudoin, Université Laval.

cub 1

cub 2

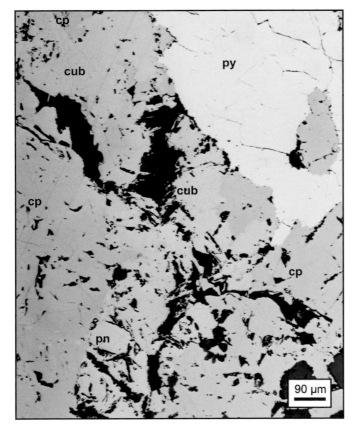

cub 3

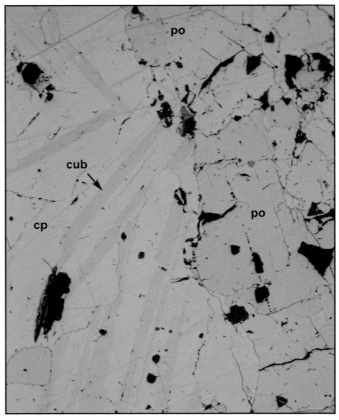

cub 4

Diamond (dia)

C

Cubic

Characteristics

Hand Specimen	
Colour	Colourless, grey, blue, green, pink, yellow
Hardness	10
Density	3.5

Distinguishing Features

Diamond is distinguished by its hardness of 10, high refractive index, adamantine lustre, and perfect cleavage in four directions. Twinning is common on octahedral crystals, and some crystal faces may be curved. Diamond is insoluble in acids and alkalis, and fluoresces blue and green. The hardness generally precludes examination of diamond in thin or polished section.

Associated Minerals

Sub-calcic Cr-Pyrope, Chrome-diopside, ilmenite, chromite, and olivine.

Mode of Occurrence

A rare mineral, diamond occurs as xenocrysts in rocks such as kimberlite, lamproite, lamprophyre, orangite, and as primary minerals in high-grade metamorphic rocks such as eclogite, harzburgite, and lherzolite. Diamond may occur in placer deposits due to its hardness and density. Diamond is also occasionally found in meteorites. Economic concentrations of diamond have been found only in kimberlite, lamproite, and placer deposits. Diamonds are generally found in association with areas of Archean crust. Notable occurrences include South Africa, Australia, and the Northwest Territories of Canada.

References

Collins A.T. (1982) Colour centers in diamond. Journal of Gemmology, v. 18, p. 37-75.
Field J.E. (1979) The properties of diamond. Academic Press. London, 674 p.
Harlow G.E. (1998) The nature of diamonds. Cambridge University Press. 278 p.
Kirkely M.B., Gurney J.J. and Levinson A.A. (1991) Age, Origin, and emplacement of diamonds:scientific advances in the last decade. Gems and Gemmology, v. 27, p. 2-25.
Richardson S.H., Gurney J.J., Erlank A.J. and Harris J.W. (1984) Origin of diamonds in old enriched mantle. Nature, v. 310, p. 198-202.
Sobolev N.V. and Shatsky V.S. (1990) Diamond inclusions in garnets from metamorphic rocks: A new environment for diamond formation. Nature, v. 343, p. 742-746.

Figures

dia 1 1.2 ct diamond in kimberlite. Mir Pipe, Russia. Specimen (S95.51) from Art Soregaroli. Photograph by Dan Marshall.

dia 2 1.5 ct diamond in kimberlite. Mir Pipe, Russia. Specimen (S95.52) from Art Soregaroli. Photograph by Dan Marshall.

dia 3 This diamond is a macle twin, with serrate laminae, ribbing, and knob-like asperities. This close-up also shows that tetragonal pits are also present. Scale is 200 microns. Electron microscope image by Tom McCandless, Ashton Mining.

dia 4 Diamond is single octahedron with triangular plates, serrate laminae and tetragonal pits. Scale is 200 microns. Electron microscope image by Tom McCandless, Ashton Mining.

Text contribution by John Armstrong (DIAND, NWT).

dia 1

dia 2

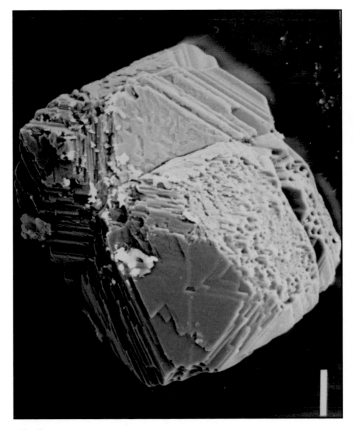

dia 3

dia 4

Digenite (dg)

Cu_9S_5 **Cubic**

Characteristics

Hand Specimen	
Colour	Blue, dark blue, black
Hardness	$2\frac{1}{2}-3$
Density	$5.5-5.7$

Polished Section			
Colour	Bluish	Cleavage	Well developed octahedral cleavage
Bireflectance	Not present	Anisotropy	Weak anomalous anisotropism
Refl (546nm)	21.3	Refl (589nm)	19.8

Distinguishing Features

In hand specimen, the blue to black colour, greyish black streak, submetallic lustre, softness, brittleness, and conchoidal fracture are diagnostic. Digenite does not generally form idiomorphic crystals, although it may display a pseudocubic crystal habit. In polished section, the copper mineral associations, bluish colour, good polish, and moderate reflectance are characteristic.

Associated Minerals

Commonly occurs intimately associated with chalcocite or covellite. May occur intergrown with bornite. Also occurs with chalcopyrite, enargite, tetrahedrite-tennantite, pyrite, galena, and sphalerite.

Mode of Occurrence

Formed under a wide range of conditions, digenite is found in hydrothermal copper deposits of primary and secondary origin, in mesothermal base metal veins of the Coeur D'Alene district, Idaho, in stratiform copper and porphyry copper deposits, and is reported from black smokers in the Mid-Atlantic Ridge, where it is secondary after chalcopyrite/isocubanite. It usually occurs in massive and granular habit disseminated with other sulphides, particularly those of copper.

References

Kojima S., Astudillo J., Rojo J., Trista D. and Hayashi K. (2003) Ore mineralogy, fluid inclusion, and stable isotopic characteristics of stratiform copper deposits in the coastal Cordillera of northern Chile. Mineralium Deposita, v. 38, p. 208-216.

Morimoto N. and Gyobu A. (1971) composition and stability of digenite. American Mineralogist, v. 56, p. 11-12.

Ossandón G., Fréraut R., Gustafson L.B., Lindsay D.D. and Zentilli M. (2001) Geology of the Chuquicamata mine: A progress report. Economic Geology, v. 96, p. 249-270.

Will G., Hinze E. and Abdelrahman A. (2002) Crystal structure analyses and refinement of digenite, $Cu_{1.8}S$ in the temperature range 20 to 500°C under controlled sulfur partial pressure. European Journal of Mineralogy, v. 14, p. 591-598.

Figures

dg 1   Digenite with pyrite from the porphyry system at the Leonard deposit, Butte. Montana. Specimen (LT 104) from Lloyd Twaites. Photograph by Dan Marshall.

dg 2   Chalcopyrite (cp) replaces and is intergrown with pyrite (py). The chalcopyrite has a rim of digenite altering to covellite. Teck Cominco specimen 43-200.5.

dg 3   Digenite (dg) replaces chalcopyrite (cp) and infills around pyrite (py). Sphalerite is replaced by digenite. Cerateppe property, Turkey. Teck Cominco specimen R91:15182. Plane polarized reflected light.

dg 1

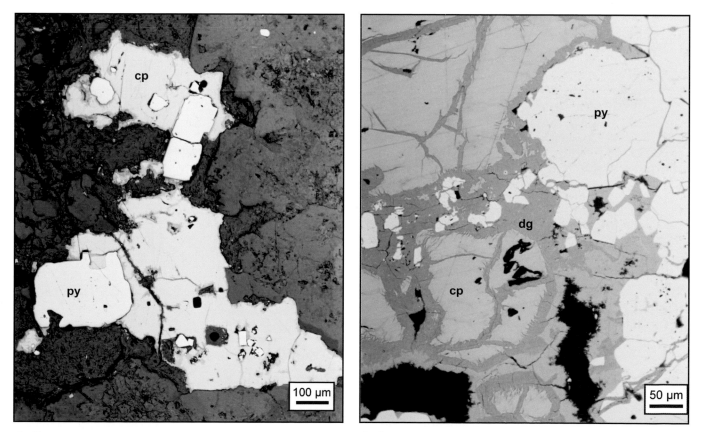

dg 2

dg 3

Enargite (ena)

Environment: Epithermal, vein, VMS, porphyry

Cu_3AsS_4

Orthorhombic

Characteristics

Hand Specimen	
Colour	Greyish black to iron black, with violet tint
Hardness	3
Density	4.4 – 4.5

Polished Section			
Colour	Pinkish grey to pinkish brown	Cleavage	{110} Perfect, {100}, {010} Distinct
Bireflectance	Distinct in oil	Anisotropy	Strong, blue, green, red, orange
Refl (546nm)	25.0 – 26.4	Refl (589nm)	25.5 – 26.8

Distinguishing Features

Characterized in hand specimen by its color, dark grey to black streak, metallic to dull lustre, lengthwise striations on crystal faces, and distinct cleavage. Twinning is common. In polished section, the light pink-brown colour and strong anisotropy are distinctive. Enargite has moderate reflectance, much higher than bornite.

Associated Minerals

Commonly associated with chalcopyrite, pyrite, bornite, tetrahedrite-tennantite, covellite, digenite, galena, and sphalerite.

Mode of Occurrence

Enargite occurs in vein and replacement deposits formed at moderate temperatures. Habit is usually massive, granular, and radiating aggregates. Twinning is common and enargite may form well-shaped crystals, characterized by pseudo-hexagonal prismatic to blocky or tabular habits, and may form a star-shaped cyclic twin. It is an important ore mineral at Butte, Montana; at the Chuquicamata porphyry copper deposit, Chile; and in several large Peruvian copper deposits.

References

Carlile J.C. and Mitchell A.H.G (1994) Magmatic arcs and associated gold and copper mineralization in Indonesia. Journal of Geochemical Exploration, v. 50, p. 91-142.

Garza R.A.P., Titley S.R. and Pimentel B.F. (2001) Geology of the Escondida porphyry copper deposit, Antofagasta region, Chile. Economic Geology, v. 96, p. 307-324.

Lambe R.N. and Rowe R.G. (1987) Volcanic history, mineralization, and alteration of the Crandon massive sulfide deposit, Wisconsin. Economic Geology, v. 82, p. 1204-1238.

Sillitoe R.H. (1983) Enargite-bearing massive sulfide deposits high in porphyry copper systems. Economic Geology, v. 78, p. 348-352.

Springer G. (1969) Compositional variations in enargite and luzonite. Mineralium Deposita, v. 4, p. 72-74.

Taylor L.G. and Bornhorst T.J. (1998) A boiling model for the formation of enargite-bearing veins in the Central City district, Colorado. The Mountain Geologist, v. 35, p. 15-22.

Figures

ena 1 Enargite crystals. Cerro de Pasco, Perú. F.O.V. 9.5 cm. Specimen from Musée de géologie René-Bureau. Photograph by Georges Beaudoin, Université Laval.

ena 2 Enargite with pyrite from the Marca Punta deposit, El Brocal, Perú. Specimen from John Hamilton. Photograph by Dan Marshall.

ena 3 Prismatic enargite (ena) with pyrite (py) and chalcopyrite (cp) inclusions. Gangue is a sugary quartz (sinter?). Marcapunta, El Brocal, Perú. Teck Cominco specimen R96:3518. Reflected light.

ena 4 Prismatic enargite (ena) and rounded grains of colusite (col) in fine grained alunite with quartz (qtz) crystals. Marcapunta, El Brocal, Perú. Teck Cominco specimen R96:3520. Reflected light.

ena 1

ena 2

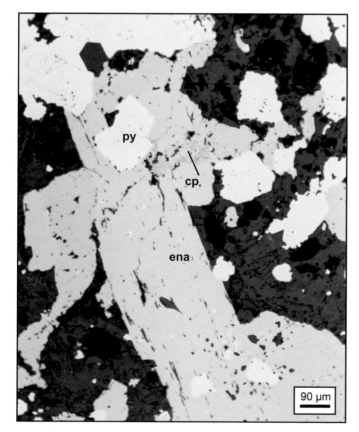

ena 3

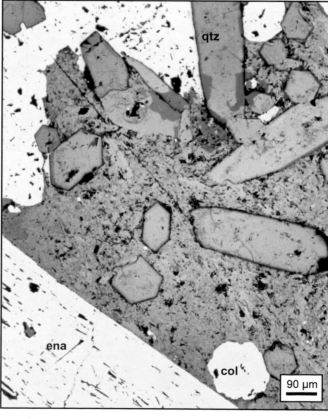

ena 4

Galena (gn)

Environment: MVT, VMS, SEDEX, vein

PbS

Cubic

Characteristics

Hand Specimen	
Colour	Lead grey, bluish tint
Hardness	2½
Density	7.4 – 7.6

Polished Section			
Colour	White	Cleavage	{100} Perfect
Bireflectance	Not present	Anisotropy	Isotropic
Refl (546nm)	42.2	Refl (589nm)	41.5

Distinguishing Features

The typically euhedral crystal habits of cube, octahedron, and combinations of the two are diagnostic, as well as perfect cleavage in four directions forming cubes. The softness, high density, lead-grey colour and streak are also characteristic. In polished section, the bright white colour (with pinkish or purplish tints), perfect cleavage {100}, usually visible as triangular pits, softness, poor polish, and moderately high reflectance are diagnostic. Impurities such as Ag will result in curved cleavage faces.

Associated Minerals

Galena is a common mineral, particularly associated with sphalerite, pyrite, chalcopyrite, tetrahedrite-tennantite, argentite, and lead sulphosalts. In addition to various sulphides, galena commonly occurs with barite, fluorite, quartz, and calcite.

Mode of Occurrence

Galena is the most important Pb ore and is present in variable amounts in many different types of ore deposits. Galena occurs in Mississippi Valley type (MVT) Pb-Zn deposits where it is associated with sphalerite, in veins, open space fillings, or replacement bodies in carbonate. Galena is the main lead mineral in Zn-Pb-Cu VMS and SEDEX deposits. When present in hydrothermal veins, it is commonly associated with silver minerals. Galena may be an important ore of Ag due to high silver contents or inclusions of silver-bearing minerals.

References

Bortnikov N.S., Dobrovolskaya M.G., Genkin A.D., Naumov V.B. and Shapenko V.V. (1995) Sphalerite-galena geothermometers: Distribution of cadmium, manganese, and the fractionation of sulphur isotopes. Economic Geology, v. 90, p. 155-180.

Fowler A.D. (1996) Self-organized banded sphalerite and branching galena in the Pine Point ore deposit, Northwest Territories. Canadian Mineralogist, v. 34, p. 1211-1222.

Hamilton J.M., Delaney D.T., Hauser R.L. and Ransom P.W. (1983) Geology of the Sullivan deposit, Kimberley, B.C. *in* Sediment-hosted Stratiform Lead-Zinc Deposits, (ed.) D.F. Sangster. Mineralogical Association of Canada, Short Course Handbook, v. 8, p. 31-38.

Huston D.L., Jablonski W. and Sie S.H. (1996) The distribution and mineral hosts of silver in eastern Australian volcanogenic massive sulfide deposits. Canadian Mineralogist, v. 34, p. 529-546.

Figures

gn 1 Specimen of Mississippi Valley type ore from the Polaris deposit, Cornwallis Island, Canada of cubic galena with minor sphalerite in sparry dolomite. F.O.V. 73.6 mm x 92 mm. Specimen from Jerry Katchen and photograph by P. Adamo.

gn 2 Specimen of Mississippi Valley type ore from the Nanisivik mine, Baffin Island, Canada of banded fine-grain sphalerite and galena. F.O.V. 56 mm x 70 mm. Specimen from Jerry Katchen. Photograph by P. Adamo.

gn 3 Deformed galena showing bends and kinks in the cleavage and the characteristic triangular pits of galena in polished section. Specimen from the Simon Fraser University collection. Photograph by Dan Marshall.

gn 4 Photomicrograph of carbonate replacement type ore (San Gregorio Mine, Central Perú) showing light grey galena (gn) with triangular pits in association with sphalerite (sph), arsenopyrite (apy), and pinkish beige pyrrhotite (po). Plane reflected light. F.O.V. 1.36 mm x 1.70 mm. Specimen from Austin Gulliver. Photomicrograph by H. Mumin.

gn 1

gn 2

— 0.1 mm

gn 3

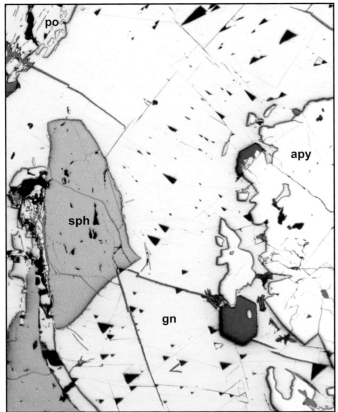

gn 4

Gersdorffite (ger)

Environment: Epithermal, vein, magmatic

NiAsS

Cubic and orthorhombic

Characteristics

Hand Specimen	
Colour	Silvery white
Hardness	5½
Density	5.9

Polished Section			
Colour	White with yellow or pink tint	Cleavage	{100} Good
Bireflectance	Not present	Anisotropy	Isotropic, some anomalous anisotropism
Refl (546nm)	45.0	Refl (589nm)	45.4

Distinguishing Features

In hand specimen, gersdorffite is silvery white and quickly tarnishes dull and dark. Hardness and specific gravity are greater than average for metallic minerals. It closely resembles arsenopyrite, cobaltite, and skutterudite. In polished section, gersdorffite is white with pink tints, isotropic, has high reflectance, and takes a good polish.

Associated Minerals

Occurs with pyrrhotite, pentlandite, magnetite, chalcopyrite, silver, skutterudite, bismuth, arsenopyrite, and cobaltite. May also occur as intergrowths with nickeline and associated minerals. Note: gersdorffite forms a solid solution series with cobaltite but is much more rare than the cobaltite end member.

Mode of Occurrence

Occurs as single euhedral to subhedral crystals and crystal groups, as well as in massive anhedral masses with pyrrhotite, pentlandite, and magnetite. Gersdorffite can occur in both magmatic sulphide deposits (Sudbury and Thompson, Canada) and in low- to moderate-temperature veins (Cobalt, Canada).

References

Gaines R.V., Skinner H.C.W., Foord E.E., Mason B. and Rozenzweig A. (1997) Dana's new mineralogy. 8th edition. J. Wiley and Sons Inc., New York, 1817 p.

Petruk W., Harris D.C. and Stewart J.M. (1971) Characteristics of the arsenides, sulpharsenides, and antimonides. Canadian Mineralogist, v. 11, p. 150-186.

Vokes F.M. and Strand G.S. (1982) Atoll texture in minerals of the cobaltite-gersdorffite series from the Raipas Mine, Finmark, Norway. in Ore genesis: The State of the Art, (ed.) G. Arnstutz et al., Springer-Verlag, Berlin, Germany, p. 118-130.

Wagner T. and Lorenz J. (2002) Mineralogy of complex Co-Ni-Bi vein mineralization, Bieber Deposit, Spessart, Germany. Mineralogical Magazine, v. 66, p. 385-407.

Yund R.A. (1962) The system Ni-As-S; phase relations and mineralogical significance. American Journal of Science, v. 260, p. 761-782.

Figures

ger 1   Vein and disseminations of pyrrhotite and pentlandite in massive and crystalline (octahedra) gersdorffite (grey). Specimen from Art Soregaroli. Photograph by Dan Marshall.

ger 2   Massive gersdorffite (grey) enclosing pyrrhotite (light grey) and amphibole (black). Thompson deposit, Thompson, Manitoba. Edge of coin is 1.7 cm. Specimen from Art Soregaroli. Photograph by Dan Marshall.

ger 3   Core of nickeline (nic) has a two-phase (2-grey) alteration rind of differing compositions of gersdorffite (ger). Teck Cominco specimen R90:258. Metla, British Columbia. Plane polarized reflected light.

0.5 cm

ger 1

ger 2

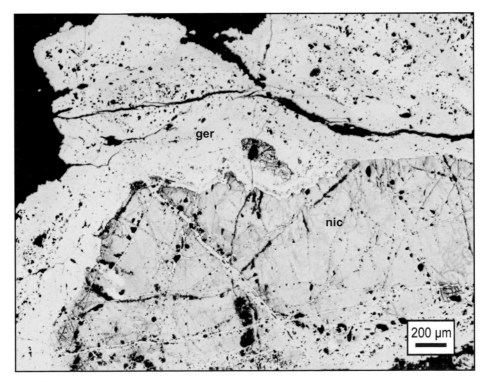

ger

nic

200 μm

ger 3

Goethite (goe)

Environment: Secondary, vein

FeO · OH

Orthorhombic

Characteristics

Hand Specimen	
Colour	Metallic black, yellowish to dark red-brown
Hardness	5 – 5½
Density	3.3 – 4.3

Polished Section			
Colour	Grey, with bluish tint	Cleavage	{010} Perfect
Bireflectance	Weak, distinct in oil	Anisotropy	Distinct, grey-blue to grey-yellow, brown
Refl (546nm)	13.2 – 14.5	Refl (589nm)	12.7 – 13.9

Distinguishing Features

Most commonly found in massive, botryoidal, or earthy habits, goethite is blackish brown or reddish to yellowish brown in hand specimen. The yellowish brown to orange-brown streak distinguishes it from the brownish red streak of hematite. In polished section, goethite is grey with bluish tints. It has low reflectance, distinct anistropism, and abundant red, orange, or yellow internal reflections.

Associated Minerals

Associated with siderite, hematite, pyrite, pyrrhotite, manganese-oxides, sphalerite, galena, fluorite, barite, limonite, jarosite, and chalcopyrite.

Mode of Occurrence

Goethite is a common ore of iron. It typically forms under oxidizing conditions as a weathering product of iron-bearing minerals, such as siderite, magnetite, pyrite, etc., and as such can be found anywhere these minerals are exposed to oxidizing conditions. It can precipitate in marine, lacustrine, and terrestrial environments and forms the weathered "gossan" observed over many metalliferous deposits. Geothite was a principal ore mineral at the Steeprock and Caland mines at Atikokan, Ontario, where it was secondary after pyrite. Goethite's most typical habits are as porous colloform bands with radiating fibres, or as porous pseudomorphs after pyrite and other Fe-bearing minerals.

References

Dorr J. (1964) Supergene iron ores of Minas Gerais, Brazil. Economic Geology, v. 59, p. 1203-1240.

Oyman T., Minareci F. and Pikin Ö. (2003) Efemçukuru B-rich epithermal gold deposit (Zmir, Turkey). Ore Geology Reviews, v. 23, p. 35-53.

Ramberg I.B. (1969) Lepidocrocite at Rossvatn, North Norway, an example of pseudomorphism after pyrite cubes. Norsk Geologisk Tidsskrift, v. 49, p. 251-256.

Schweigart H. (1965) Genesis of the iron ores of the Pretoria series, South Africa. Economic Geology, v. 60, p. 269-298.

Ucurum A., Larson L.T. and Boztag D. (1996) Geology, geochemistry, and petrology of the alkaline subvolcanic trachyte-hosted iron deposit in the Karakuz area, northwestern Hekimhan-Malatya, Turkey. International Geology Review, v. 38, p. 995-1005.

Figures

goe 1 Botryoidal, mammillary goethite on an earthy brown amorphous substrate. Weathered zone, Ishpeming, Michigan. F.O.V. ~8.0 cm x 10.0 cm. Submitted by A.H. Mumin and P.J. Adamo, Brandon University.

goe 2 Columnar, stalactitic and vuggy goethite showing black metallic to earthy grey-brown colour. Weathered zone, Biwabik, Minnesota. F.O.V. ~2.9 cm x 3.6 cm. Submitted by A.H. Mumin and P.J. Adamo, Brandon University.

goe 3 Botryoidal goethite (light and dark red) in plane polarized light. White and blue are holes in the specimen.

goe 4 Same specimen as in **goe 3** in reflected light under partly crossed polars showing the characteristic blue and orange anisotropism. Specimen from the Simon Fraser University collection. Photograph by Dan Marshall.

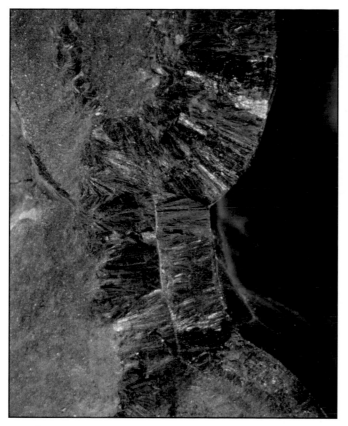

goe 1

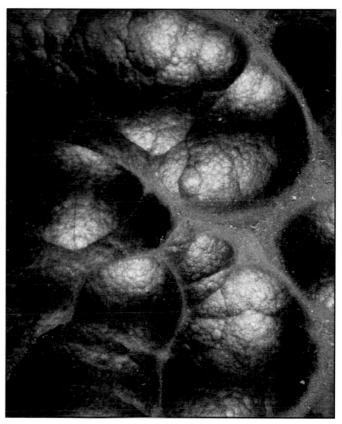

goe 2

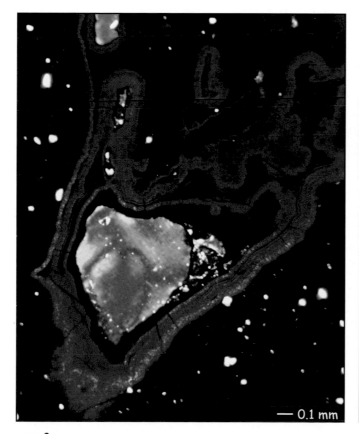

goe 3

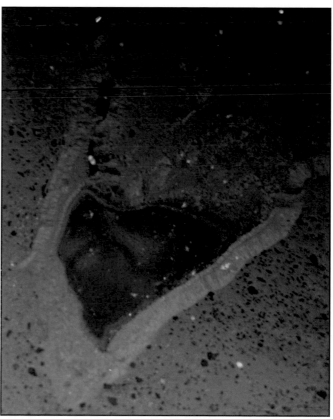

goe 4

— 0.1 mm

Gold (au)

Environment: Mesothermal, epithermal, vein, VMS placer, IOCG, porphyry and intrusion related

Au   Cubic

Characteristics

Hand Specimen	
Colour	Shades of yellow
Hardness	2½ – 3
Density	19.3 (pure)

Polished Section			
Colour	Bright golden yellow	Cleavage	Absent
Bireflectance	Not present	Anisotropy	Isotropic
Refl (546nm)	65.0	Refl (589nm)	72.3

Distinguishing Features

In hand specimen, the bright golden yellow colour, resistance to tarnish, metallic lustre, hackly fracture, malleability, and very high density are diagnostic. In reflected light, the golden colour, very high reflectance, softness, and extinction behaviour (never completely extinguishes under crossed nicols, with typical greenish tints) are characteristic. The presence of Ag alloyed with the gold lightens the colour to more whitish yellow and increases the reflectance. The term "fineness" refers to the purity of the gold. When gold contains greater than 20% silver it is referred to as electrum, which commonly also contains some copper and trace metals.

Associated Minerals

In quartz veins with pyrite, arsenopyrite, galena, sphalerite, stibnite, tellurides, chalcopyrite, pyrrhotite, Ag-bearing minerals, Bi-bearing minerals, scheelite, tourmaline, and carbonates. In massive sulphide deposits with pyrite, chalcopyrite, galena, and sphalerite. In placer deposits with detrital heavy minerals.

Mode of Occurrence

Gold occurs in massive nuggets in placer deposits, and as disseminated grains, wires, laminae, and rarely as crystals, in a variety of hydrothermal deposit types. Economic concentrations occur in a variety of ore deposit types including mesothermal (Timmins camp), the often debated sediment-hosted type (Witwatersrand), porphyry (Grasberg), high- and low-sulphidation epithermal, intrusion-related (Pogo, Alaska), gold-rich VMS (Eskay Creek, British Columbia) and Carlin-type.

References

Barrett T.J. and Sherlock R.L. (1996) Geology, lithogeochemistry and volcanic setting of the Eskay Creek Au-Ag-Cu-Zn deposit, northwestern British Columbia. Exploration and Mining Geology, v. 5, p. 339-368.

Kerrich R., Goldfarb R., Groves D. and Garwin S. (2000) The geodynamics of world-class gold deposits: Characteristics, space-time distribution, and origins. in Gold in 2000, (ed.) S.G. Hagemann and P.E. Brown, Reviews in Economic Geology, v. 13, p. 501-551.

Knight J.B., Mortensen J.K. and Morison S.R. (1999) Lode and placer gold composition in the Klondike District, Yukon Territory, Canada: Implications for the nature and genesis of Klondike placer and lode gold deposits. Economic Geology, v. 94, p. 649-664.

Michel D. and Giuliani G. (1996) Habit and composition of gold grains in quartz veins from greenstone belts: Implications for mechanisms of precipitation of gold. Canadian Mineralogist, v. 34, p. 513-528.

Sheets R.W., Craig J.R. and Bodnar R.J. (1995) Composition and occurrence of electrum at the Morning Star Deposit, San Bernardino County, California: Evidence for remobilization of gold and silver. Canadian Mineralogist, v. 33, p. 137-151.

Figures

au 1   Gold in arsenopyrite-calcite-quartz vein. Privateer Mine, Zeballos, British Columbia. Specimen from Adolf Aichmeier. Photograph by Dan Marshall. Coin diameter is 2.1 cm.

au 2   Gold in matrix, Lamaque deposit, Quebec. Specimen S94.86 from Art Soregaroli. Photograph by Dan Marshall.

au 3   Gold (au) and tennantite (tn) occurring as inclusions in arsenopyrite (apy) and silicates from the Con Mine, Northwest Territories. Plane polarized reflected light. Specimen from Simon Fraser University collection. Photograph by Dan Marshall.

au 4   Native gold (au) occurs as subhedral crystals within a quartz veinlet that cross-cuts massive arsenopyrite (apy). The arsenopyrite itself hosts approximately 10 ppm Au in solid solution. Goldenridge Deposit, (Tanzania) of Barrick Gold Corporation. Submitted by Nicki McKay, SGS-Lakefield Research Limited. Plane polarized reflected light. Photograph by Dan Marshall.

au 1

au 2

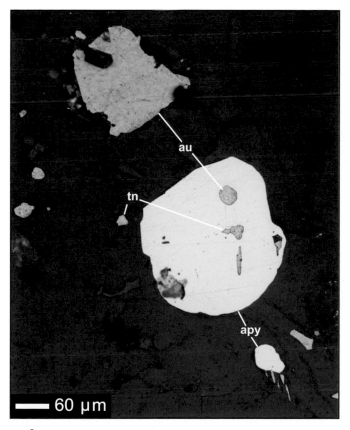

au 3

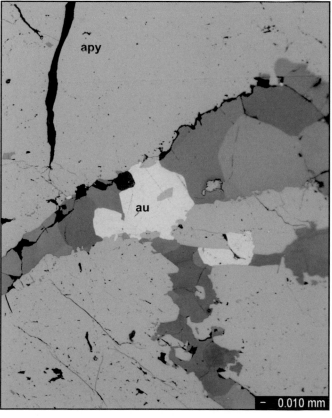

au 4

Graphite (gr)

Environment: Metamorphic, magmatic, vein

C

Hexagonal

Characteristics

Hand Specimen	
Colour	Grey metallic
Hardness	1 – 2
Density	2.1 – 2.3

Polished Section			
Colour	Light to dark grey	Cleavage	{0001} Perfect
Bireflectance	Very strong, brownish grey to greyish black	Anisotropy	Very strong, straw yellow to brown or violet grey
Refl (546nm)	7.4 – 7.5	Refl (589nm)	20.5 – 21.5

Distinguishing Features

Characteristically dark grey to black colour and streak, dull metallic lustre, greasy feel, flattened crystals, tabular, hexagonal plates, perfect basal cleavage, commonly massive, foliated, or granular in hand specimen. In polished section, graphite displays small plates, flakes, or sheaf-like aggregates. Its greyish black colour, low reflectance, and strong anisotropy (with quite bright but only slightly coloured yellowish tints) are characteristic. Graphite may be confused with molybdenite; the latter is denser and has a silver-blue streak. In polished section, the colour of molybdenite is darker than that of graphite, and molybdenite polarizes in pinkish rather than yellowish tints. Graphite is difficult to polish and may show undulose extinction due to strain.

Associated Minerals

Found in marble, paragneiss, pelitic schist, quartzite, magnetite-graphite iron-formation, amphibolite, metamorphosed coal beds and other metamorphosed carbon-rich rocks. It may occur as inclusions in sphalerite, pyrite, magnetite, and pyrrhotite. In hydrothermal veins, graphite is associated with quartz, biotite, K-feldspar, tourmaline, apatite, pyrite, and titanite.

Mode of Occurrence

A common mineral, graphite occurs in many metamorphic rocks, either contact or regional, in which it is thought to have formed through metamorphism of organic material. It also occurs in igneous rocks, including pegmatite and some veins, and may also occur in some iron meteorites as graphite nodules. Most commercial deposits of natural graphite are of metamorphic origin. Economic deposits may contain crystalline flake, microcrystalline, or amorphous graphite. The coarser flakes are the more valuable.

References

Barrenechea J.F., Luque F.J., Rodas M. and Pasteris J.D. (1997) Vein-type graphite in Jurassic volcanic rocks of the external zone of the Betic Cordillera, southern Spain. Canadian Mineralogist, v. 35, p. 1379-1390.

Hewitt D.F. (1965) Graphite in Ontario. Ontario Department of Mines, Industrial Minerals Report 20, 66 p.

Pirajno F., Thomassen B. and Dawes P.R. (2003) Copper–gold occurrences in the Palaeoproterozoic Inglefield mobile belt, northwest Greenland: A new mineralisation style?. Ore Geology Reviews, v. 22, p. 225-249.

Simandl G.J. and Kenan W.M. (1997) Crystalline Flake Graphite. in Geological Fieldwork 1997. British Columbia Ministry of Employment and Investment, Paper 1998-1, p. 1-3.

Figures

gr 1 Scanned slab of strongly schistose scapolite-graphite-clinopyroxene paragneiss from the Hartwell prospect, Quebec. Typical bluish grey graphite makes up 3 to 15 percent of the specimen. Photograph submitted by George Simandl, British Columbia Geological Survey.

gr 2 Graphite. Unknown locality. Coin edge is 2.2 cm. Specimen (S52.33) from Art Soregaroli. Photograph by Dan Marshall

gr 3 Coarse flake of graphite. The polished section cross-cuts the flake showing the undulating extinction and silver-grey colour of the graphite. Plane polarized reflected light.

gr 4 Corresponding photograph showing the similar anisotropic colours. Reflected light, partially crossed polars. Nunavut, Canada. Specimen contributed by Nicki McKay, SGS-Lakefield Research Limited. Photograph by Dan Marshall.

gr 1

0.6 cm

gr 2

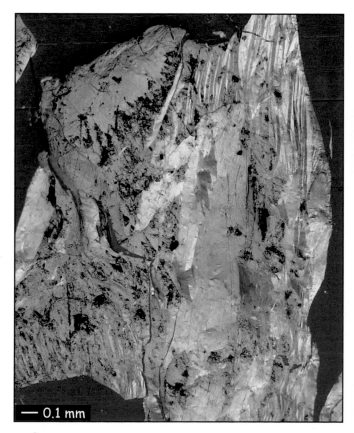

— 0.1 mm

gr 3

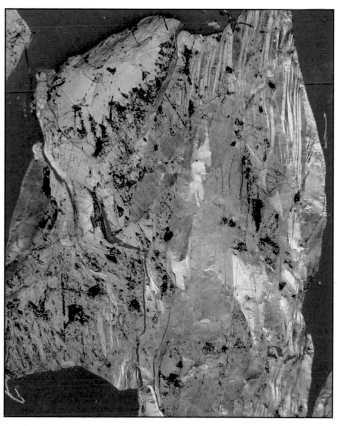

gr 4

Hematite (hem)

Environment: Secondary, magmatic, epithermal porphyry, IOCG, skarn, sedimentary

Fe_2O_3 Hexagonal

Characteristics

Hand Specimen	
Colour	Red-brown (earthy), or metallic (specular)
Hardness	5½ – 6½
Density	5.2 – 5.3

Polished Section			
Colour	Grey-white with bluish tint	Cleavage	Absent; {0001},{1012} only partly due to twinning
Bireflectance	Weak	Anisotropy	Distinct, grey-blue, grey-yellow
Refl (546nm)	27.0 – 30.6	Refl (589nm)	26.0 – 29.7

Distinguishing Features

Hematite has variable colour and lustre depending on its habit. It ranges from metallic lustre and steel or silvery grey to black, in its crystalline (specular) form, to red to brown colour and dull lustre when in its earthy habit. All forms of hematite have a characteristic reddish brown streak. In addition to its earthy and specular forms, botryoidal habit is common. In polished section, hematite is white to grey-white with moderate reflectance and distinct anisotropism. Hematite displays deep red internal reflections. It is also difficult to polish due to its lamellar texture.

Associated Minerals

Common as exsolution lenses or lamellae in ilmenite or magnetite, or as a host to lamellae of the same. It is also commonly associated with pyrite, chalcopyrite, bornite, rutile, chromite, cassiterite, goethite, and sphalerite, and with siderite, limonite, and quartz.

Mode of Occurrence

Hematite is the most important ore of iron and is also a common alteration mineral. Economically significant concentrations of hematite occur in Precambrian rocks throughout the world. These deposits occur in enormous masses in regionally metamorphosed siliceous Fe-rich sedimentary rocks, where residual accumulations of hematite and goethite have developed by leaching of associated silica by natural processes. It occurs in contact metamorphic deposits and as an important phase in some iron-oxide-Cu-Au (IOCG) deposits. It is also found as an alteration mineral in a wide variety of mineralizing environments.

References

Beukes N.J., Gutzmer J. and Mukhopadhyay J. (2003) The geology and genesis of high-grade hematite iron ore deposits. Institution of Mining and Metallurgy, Transactions, v. 112, p. 18-25.

Dalstra H., Harding T., Riggs T. and Taylor D. (2003) Banded iron formation hosted high-grade hematite deposits, a coherent group? Institution of Mining and Metallurgy, Transactions, v. 112, p. 68-72.

Gross, G.A. (1965) Geology of iron deposits in Canada. Volume 1. General Geology and Evaluation of Iron Deposits. Geological Survey of Canada, Economic Geology Report No. 22, 181 p.

Rosiere C.A., Siemes H., Quade H., Brokmeier H.G. and Jansen E.M. (2001) Microstructures, textures and deformation mechanisms in hematite. Journal of Structural Geology, v. 23, no. 9, p. 1429-1440.

Xu G. and Lin X. (2000) Geology and geochemistry of the Changlongshan skarn iron deposit, Anhui Province, China. Ore Geology Reviews, v. 16, p. 91-106.

Figures

hem 1 Specular and earthy hematite. Coin diameter is 1.8 cm. Specimen from the Simon Fraser University collection.

hem 2 Botryoidal hematite. Beckermet, Cumbria, Great Britain. Specimen (#S83.17) from Art Soregaroli.

hem 3 Hematite in polished thin section displaying bent crystals. Specimen from the Simon Fraser University collection. Plane polarized reflected light.

hem 4 Hematite as in **hem 3** showing corresponding anisotropy under partly crossed polarized light.

Photographs by Dan Marshall.

hem 1

hem 2

— 0.1 mm

hem 3

hem 4

Ilmenite (ilm)

Environment: Magmatic, metamorphic

$FeTiO_3$

Trigonal

Characteristics

Hand Specimen	
Colour	Black to brown
Hardness	5½ – 6
Density	4.7

Polished Section			
Colour	Pinkish brown		Absent
Bireflectance	Distinct, pinkish brown to dark brown	**Anisotropy**	Strong, greenish grey to brownish grey
Refl (546nm)	18.0 – 19.7	**Refl (589nm)**	18.0 – 19.9

Distinguishing Features

In hand specimen, ilmenite usually forms thick tabular crystals, is dark brown to black with a black-brown streak, and has a dull to metallic lustre. It may be slightly magnetic and lamellar twinning is common. It is commonly altered to "leucoxene", a whitish to light brown alteration product containing titanite and Ti-oxides (including rutile and brookite). In polished section, its distinct pinkish brown to dark brown anisotropism and common exsolution lamellae of hematite or magnetite are diagnostic.

Associated Minerals

Occurs with magnetite, hematite, apatite, rutile, pyrite, pyrrhotite, chromite, and tantalite.

Mode of Occurrence

Ilmenite is an important ore of titanium. Ilmenite occurs with magnetite in placer deposits, as a layered segregation in anorthositic and ultramafic rocks, and as a common accessory mineral in metamorphic and igneous rocks. Ilmenite also occurs in xenoliths in kimberlite pipes and is an important indicator mineral for diamond exploration.

References

Barksdale J. (1966) Titanium: Its Occurrence, Chemistry and Technology. Ronald Press, New York, 691 p.

Buddington A.F. and Lindsley D.H. (1964) Iron-titanium oxide minerals and synthetic equivalents. Journal of Petrology, v. 5, p. 310-357.

Diot H., Bolle O., Lambert J-M., Launeau P. and Duchesne J-C. (2003) The Tellnes ilmenite deposit (Rogaland, South Norway); magnetic and petrofabric evidence for emplacement of a Ti-enriched noritic crystal mush in a fracture zone. Journal of Structural Geology, v. 25, p. 481-501.

Jiang S.Y., Palmer M.R. and Slack J.F. (1996) Mn-rich ilmenite from the Sullivan Pb-Zn-Ag deposit, British Columbia. Canadian Mineralogist, v. 34, p 29-36.

Windley B.F., Herd R.K. and Ackermand D. (1989) Geikielite and ilmenite in Archean meta-ultramafic rocks, Fiskenaesset, West Greenland. European Journal of Mineralogy, v. 1, p. 427-437.

Figures

ilm 1   The ilmenite crystals are tabular and rounded. The enclosing matrix has been removed. The specimen is approximately 4 cm across. Faraday Prospect, Bancroft, Ontario. Photograph by Mark Mauthner.

ilm 2   Ilmenite, Simon Fraser University collection. Photograph by Holly Keyes.

ilm 3   Ilmenite in polished thin section with some lamellae of magnetite.

ilm 4   Same view as in **ilm 3** showing corresponding anisotropy, reddish brown. The magnetite lamellae are not anisotropic. Simon Fraser University collection. Photograph by Dan Marshall.

ilm 1

ilm 2

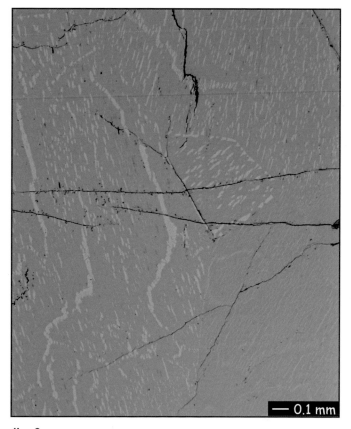

ilm 3

1 cm

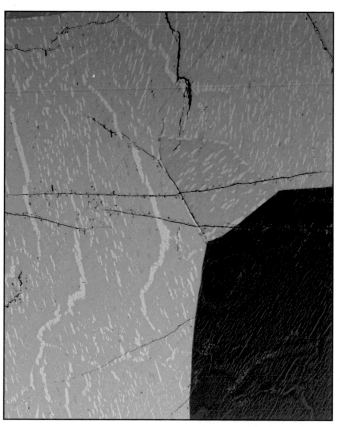

ilm 4

0.1 mm

Jamesonite (jm)

Environment: Epithermal, vein, VMS

$Pb_4FeSb_6S_{14}$

Monoclinic

Characteristics

Hand Specimen	
Colour	Steel grey to grayish black
Hardness	2 – 3
Density	5.5 – 6.0

Polished Section			
Colour	White	Cleavage	{001} Perfect
Bireflectance	Strong, white to yellow-green	Anisotropy	Strong, grey, tan, brown, blue
Refl (546nm)	33.8 – 39.7	Refl (589nm)	33.0 – 38.5

Distinguishing Features

Jamesonite is dark grey, has a metallic lustre, is very soft, has perfect cleavage perpendicular to its length, and commonly forms needle-, hair-, or lath-like crystals and radiating masses. The crystals are very brittle and not flexible as is the case for boulangerite. Polysynthetic twins are parallel to crystal elongation. In polished section, strong grey, tan, brown, blue anisotropism and white-yellow-green bireflectance are all characteristic of jamesonite. Twinning is common unlike boulangerite, which never exhibits twinning.

Associated Minerals

Associated with other lead sulphosalts (e.g. boulangerite), galena, pyrite, stibnite, sphalerite, and arsenopyrite.

Mode of Occurrence

Forms in hydrothermal settings under low to medium temperatures and pressures, generally a paragenetically late mineral in Pb-Ag-Zn, Au-Sb, and Sn-Pb-Ag ore veins.

References

Chang L., Li X. and Zheng C. (1987) The jamesonite-benavidesite series. Canadian Mineralogist, v. 25, p. 667-672.

Cook N.J., Spry P.G. and Vokes F.M. (1998) Mineralogy and textural relationships among sulphosalts and related minerals in the Bleikvassli Zn-Pb-(Cu) deposit, Nordland, Norway. Mineralium Deposita, v. 34, p. 35-56.

Gvozdev V.I. (2002) The lead-antimony-bismuth mineralization in ores of the Agylki skarn-scheelite-sulfide deposit (Yakutiya, Russia). Geology Ore Deposits, v. 44, p. 300-311.

Matsushita Y. and Ueda Y. (2003) Structure and physical properties of 1D magnetic chalcogenide, jamesonite ($FePb_4Sb_6S_{14}$). Inorganic Chemistry, v. 42, p. 7830-7838.

Figures

jm 1 Jamesonite with quartz (spheroids) and pyrite crystals. Santa Rita deposit, Zacatecas, Mexico. Specimen (S99.47) from Art Soregaroli. Photograph by Dan Marshall.

jm 2 Acicular jamesonite in vug in pyrite-quartz-sphalerite host. Specimen number (S93.81) from Art Soregaroli. Photograph by Dan Marshall.

jm 3 Photomicrograph of an aggregate of jamesonite grains (location unknown). Plane reflected light. F.O.V. 1.4 mm x 1.7 mm. Submitted by A.H. Mumin and C.G. Couëslan, Brandon University, Manitoba.

jm 4 Photomicrograph of **jm 3** in reflected light with crossed polars.

jm 1

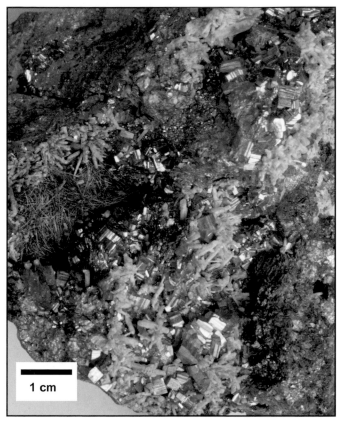

jm 2

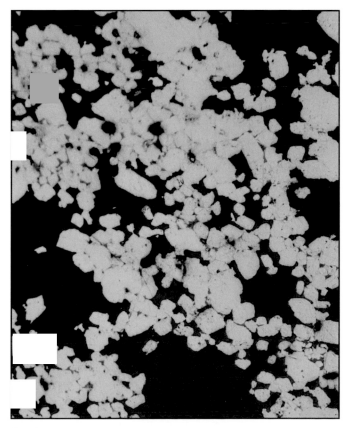

jm 3

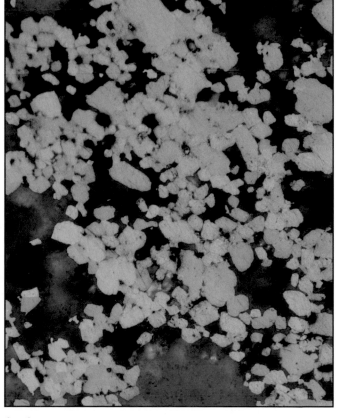

jm 4

Magnetite (mag)

Environment: Magmatic, skarn, epithermal, IOCG, sedimentary

Fe_3O_4

Cubic

Characteristics

Hand Specimen	
Colour	Iron black
Hardness	6
Density	5.2

Polished Section			
Colour	Grey with brownish tint	Cleavage	{111} Imperfect
Bireflectance	Not present	Anisotropy	Isotropic, slight anomalous anisotropism
Refl (546nm)	20.4	Refl (589nm)	20.6

Distinguishing Features

Magnetite is strongly magnetic. It is black, has a black streak, and a dull metallic lustre. It is most commonly found in massive to granular habit and when crystalline typically forms octahedra. It often contains exsolution or oxidation lamellae of hematite and lamellae of ilmenite are also common.

Associated Minerals

Magnetite is associated with a wide variety of minerals, particularly ilmenite, hematite, pyrrhotite, pyrite, pentlandite, chalcopyrite, bornite, sphalerite, and galena. Magnetite alters to hematite and goethite.

Mode of Occurrence

Magnetite is a common mineral and is associated with many ore-deposit environments. Occurrences in banded iron formations (BIF) can be a primary source of iron ore. It also occurs as laminations, resulting from segregation, or by crystal settling in the magmatic environment, such as in the Bushveld complex, SA. Magnetite is more common in mafic igneous rocks and may contain appreciable amounts of titanium. Magnetite also occurs in economic concentrations in oxidized-skarn deposits, occurring with sulphides, W, and P, and is massive to semi-massive in some IOCG deposits (e.g. el Laco, Chile). Magnetite also occurs as disseminations or veins within alteration haloes and is a common constituent of biotite-rich potassic alteration in porphyry deposits, such as at Island Copper, British Columbia. It is common in the copper-rich part of VMS systems, and as a high-temperature alteration product. Magnetite-bearing rocks can also provide favourable hosts for gold mineralization, for example Lupin, Northwest Territories.

References

Galley A.G., Jonasson I.R. and Watkinson D.H. (2000) Magnetite-rich calc-silicate alteration in relation to synvolcanic intrusion at the Ansil volcanogenic massive sulphide deposit, Rouyn-Noranda, Quebec, Canada. Mineralium Deposita, v. 35, p. 619-637.

Hoatson D.M. and Sun S-S. (2002) Archean layered mafic-ultramafic intrusions in the west Pilbara Craton, Western Australia: A synthesis of some of the oldest orthomagmatic mineralizing systems in the world. Economic Geology, v. 97, p. 847-872.

Sillitoe R.H. and Burrows D.R. (2002) New field evidence for bearing on the origin of the El-Laco magnetite deposit, northern Chile. Economic Geology, v. 97, p. 1101-1109.

Travisany V., Henriquez F. and Nystroem J.O. (1995) Magnetite lava flows in the Pleito-Melon District of the Chilean iron belt. Economic Geology, v. 90, p. 438-444.

Figures

mag 1 Magnetite on calcite from skarn. Sims claim, Lemhi Co., Idaho. Specimen (S61.41) from Art Soregaroli. Photograph by Dan Marshall.

mag 2 Magnetite with calcite and Fe-oxide (pink). Sims claim, Lemhi Co., Idaho. Specimen (S61.41) from Art Soregaroli. Photography by Dan Marshall.

mag 3 Magnetite (mag) is replaced by chalcopyrite (cp) with bornite (bn). Salobo deposit, Para State, Brazil. Teck Cominco specimen R99:1135. Reflected light.

mag 4 Hexagonal to rounded magnetite (mag) molded by pyrrhotite (po) and chalcopyrite (cp). Blue Lake, Quebec. F.O.V. 2 mm. Submitted by Georges Beaudoin, Université Laval.

mag 1

mag 2

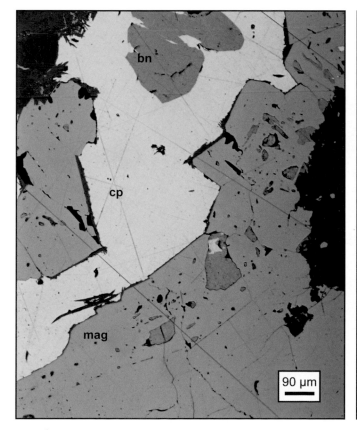

mag 3

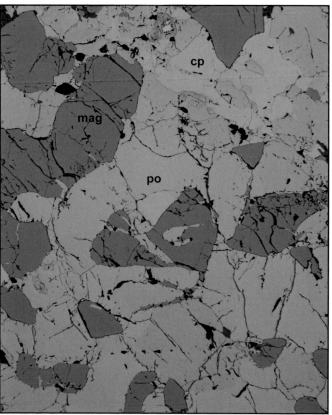

mag 4

Malachite (mal)

Environment: Secondary, porphyry

$Cu_2(OH)_2CO_3$

Monoclinic

Characteristics

Hand Specimen	
Colour	Green
Hardness	3½ – 4
Density	3.9 – 4.0

Polished Section			
Colour	Green	Cleavage	{001} Imperfect
Bireflectance	Distinct	Anisotropy	Strong
Refl (546nm)	Low	Refl (589nm)	Low

Distinguishing Features

In hand specimen, the green colour and banding, pale green streak, dull to vitreous lustre, conchoidal fracture, and effervescence in HCl are characteristic. Habit is commonly botryoidal, but can also be granular, massive, and crustiform. In thin section, the strong yellowish green pleochroism is distinctive. In polished section, malachite is grey with low reflectance and strong anisotropism that can be masked by abundant green internal reflections.

Associated Minerals

Generally occurs in association with one or many other copper minerals, such as native copper, chalcopyrite, cuprite, azurite, and chrysocolla.

Mode of Occurrence

May occur in any copper-bearing deposit even if there are only traces of copper. Far more abundant than azurite, malachite forms by the reaction of Cu-bearing solutions with carbonate minerals. Typically it occurs as crystalline aggregates or crusts, commonly growth-zoned, like agates. It may also occur as botryoidal clusters of radiating crystals, and as mammillary aggregates. Single crystals and clusters of distinguishable crystals occur, but when present they are typically acicular to prismatic. It also occurs as pseudomorphs after azurite crystals, which are generally more tabular in shape. Malachite is commonly found in the oxidized portions of porphyry copper, copper skarn, and sedimentary copper deposits.

References

Cook R.B. (2001) Malachite; Shaba region, Democratic Republic of Congo. Rocks and Minerals, v. 76, p. 326-331.

Graeme R.W. (1997) The supergene copper minerals of Bisbee, Arizona. Mineralogical Record, v. 28, p. 55.

Kelm U., Pincheira M., Oyarzun J. and Sucha V. (2001) Combarbala advanced argillic alteration zone, Chile: geology, geochemistry, mineralogy and mineralization potential. Transactions of the Institution of Mining and Metallurgy, Section B, v. 110, p. 91-102.

Melchiorre E.B., Criss R.E. and Rose T.P. (1999) Oxygen and carbon isotope study of natural and synthetic malachite. Economic Geology, v. 94, p. 245-259.

Figures

mal 1 Pastel and darker green concentric to colloform malachite overgrowing a vuggy core with minor Fe-oxide staining. Locality unknown. F.O.V. ~6.4 cm x 8.0 cm.

mal 2 Detail showing crystalline malachite with blue azurite veining from Arizona. Cut face. F.O.V. ~1.1 cm x 1.4 cm.

mal 3 Photomicrograph of **mal 2** showing green to pale yellow felted to amorphous malachite. Polished thin section, plane polarized transmitted light. F.O.V. ~0.68 mm x 0.85 mm.

mal 4 Photomicrograph of **mal 2** showing green amorphous to felted malachite with minor yellow amorphous malachite and blue azurite. Polished thin section, plane polarized transmitted light. F.O.V. ~0.68 mm x 0.85 mm.

Photographs submitted by P.J. Adamo and A.H. Mumin, Brandon University.

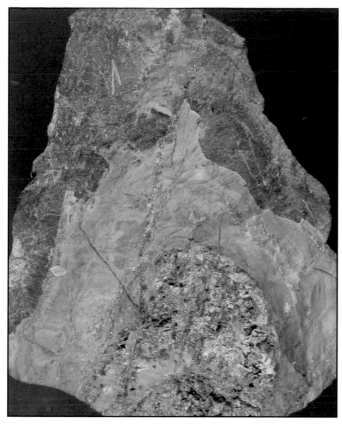

mal 1

mal 2

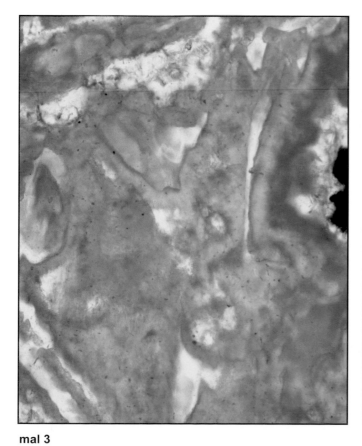

mal 3

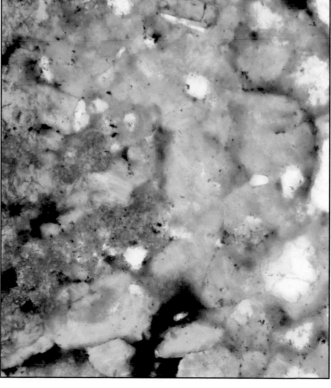

mal 4

Marcasite (mrc)

Environment: SEDEX, MVT, epithermal, vein, secondary

FeS_2

Orthorhombic

Characteristics

Hand Specimen	
Colour	Brassy, pale to creamy yellow
Hardness	6 – 6½
Density	4.8+

Polished Section			
Colour	Yellowish white with slight pinkish to greenish tint	Cleavage	{110} Poor
Bireflectance	Strong, brownish, yellowish green	Anisotropy	Strong, blue, green-yellow, purple-grey
Refl (546nm)	48.8 – 55.4	Refl (589nm)	49.0 – 53.8

Distinguishing Features

Marcasite is a polymorph of pyrite and can easily be confused with pyrite in hand specimen. It is brassy pale yellow, commonly with a greenish tint, it has a greenish black streak, oxidizes readily in air, and may produce a detectable sulphur smell, and tarnishes quickly to a darker colour. It is only readily distinguishable from pyrite when in its distinctive crystal habit (e.g. "cockscomb" crystals), which are radiating tabular twinned crystals. In polished section, the yellow-white colour, distinct bireflectance, high reflectance, strong blue to yellowish anisotropism, lamellar texture, and common twinning are diagnostic.

Associated Minerals

Marcasite commonly occurs with pyrite but also occurs with most other sulphides including galena, sphalerite, bornite, and other minerals such as dolomite, calcite, and fluorite.

Mode of Occurrence

Marcasite forms in a variety of low-temperature environments, and commonly occurs in replacement deposits in carbonate rocks, particularly MVT deposits. It also occurs as a secondary mineral in a variety of low-temperature, near-surface, environments. It is found as massive, granular or crusty aggregates, concretions, pseudomorphs, and as crystals.

References

Drapela T. and Beran A. (1993) Reflected light examination of marcasite and löllingite. Mineralogy and Petrology, v. 48, p. 269-274.

Fleet M.E. and Mumin A.H. (1997) Gold-bearing arsenian pyrite and marcasite and arsenopyrite from Carlin Trend gold deposits and laboratory synthesis. American Mineralogist, v. 82, p. 182-193.

Murowchick J.B. (1992) Marcasite inversion and the petrographic determination of pyrite ancestry. Economic Geology v. 87, p. 1141-1152.

Pichler T., Giggenbach W.F., McInnes B.I.A., Buhl D. and Duck B. (1999) Fe sulfide formation due to seawater-gas-sediment interaction in a shallow-water hydrothermal system at Lihir Island, Papua New Guinea. Economic Geology, v. 94, p. 281-288.

Figures

mrc 1 "Cogwheel" marcasite from the Mid-Continent deposit, Picher, Oklahoma. Teck Cominco specimen T420. Photograph by Dan Marshall.

mrc 2 Photomicrograph of intergrown twinned marcasite (mrc) crystals in a vug showing a range of strong anisotropic colours and reflectivities. Specimen is from Francon Quarry, Quebec and provided by Kerry Day: Kaygeedee Minerals. Photograph in reflected light under partly crossed polars by Dan Marshall.

mrc 3 Massive marcasite (mrc) displaying typical lamellar texture with massive sphalerite (sph), which contains a large inclusion of stannite (st). Chachacomiri, Bolivia. Teck Cominco specimen R95:4038. Plane polarized reflected light.

mrc 4 Marcasite (mrc), galena (gn), sphalerite (sph) and arsenopyrite (apy). Chachacomiri, Bolivia. Teck Cominco specimen R95:4038. Plane polarized reflected light.

mrc 1

mrc 2

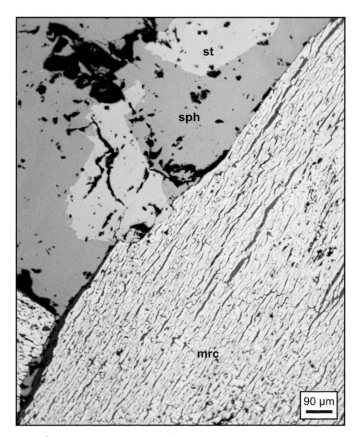

mrc 3

mrc 4

Millerite (mil)

NiS   **Hexagonal**

Characteristics

Hand Specimen	
Colour	Pale brass yellow with greenish tint
Hardness	3 – 3½
Density	5.3 – 5.5

Polished Section			
Colour	Yellow	Cleavage	{1011}, {0112} Good
Bireflectance	Distinct in oil, yellow to blue or violet	Anisotropy	Strong, lemon-yellow to blue or violet
Refl (546nm)	53.3 – 55.2	Refl (589nm)	55.2 – 57.6

Distinguishing Features

In hand specimen, it is brassy yellow, which may tarnish to a grey sometimes iridescent colour. It has a dark green to black streak, and tends to occur as very thin, brittle, hair-like, radiating acicular crystals and aggregates. It can also occur as anhedral granular masses. The light yellow colour, good polish, high reflectance, distinct bireflectance, strong yellow to blue-grey anisotropy, and tendency to form acicular crystals, commonly twinned, are distinctive. Also, it is not as brown as the higher temperature pentlandite, is more cream coloured compared with the sulphur-yellow of chalcopyrite, and is slightly more yellow than pyrite.

Associated Minerals

Occurs in association with other Ni-bearing sulphide minerals, including the linnaeite group of minerals (Co-Cu-Ni-Fe sulphides). Also may be associated with chalcopyrite, pyrite, and carbonate minerals including siderite, dolomite, ankerite, and calcite. Common as oriented intergrowths with violarite and pyrrhotite.

Mode of Occurrence

A relatively rare mineral, it has been reported from a wide variety of mineralized environments, from concretions and cavities in carbonate rocks, to association with serpentinite, and primary mafic to ultramafic-hosted magmatic sulphide. Millerite occurs in Ni-Co-Ag ores, and also forms as a low-temperature mineral in cavities and as an alteration of other nickel-rich sulphide minerals, or as crystal inclusions in other minerals. It can also form as a hydrothermal alteration product of pentlandite, therein typically assuming a granular rather than acicular habit. It has been reported in Fe-Ni meteorites.

References

Ballhaus C., Tredoux M. and Spath A. (2001) Phase relations in the Fe-Ni-Cu-PGE-S system at magmatic temperature and application to massive sulphide ores of the Sudbury Igneous Complex. Journal of Petrology, v. 42, p. 1911-1926.

Kojima S., Hanamuro T., Hayashi K., Haruna M. and Ohmoto H. (1998) Sulphide minerals in Early Archean chemical sedimentary rocks of the eastern Pilbara district, Western Australia. Mineralogy and Petrology, v. 64, p. 219-235.

Lee S.Y., Watanabe M., Hoshino K., Oomori T., Fjuioka K. and Rona P.A. (2002) First report of linnaeite (Co_3S_4) and millerite (NiS) from active submarine hydrothermal deposits: Rainbow hydrothermal field, Mid-Atlantic Ridge at 36° 14' N. Neues Jahrbuch für Mineralogie Monatshefte, v. 1, p. 1-21.

Molnar F., Watkinson D.H. and Jones P.C. (2001) Multiple hydrothermal processes in footwall units of the North Range, Sudbury Igneous Complex, Canada, and implications for the genesis of vein-type Cu-Ni-PGE deposits. Economic Geology, v. 96, p. 1645-1670.

Figures

mil 1 Fibrous, acicular millerite selvages (golden bronze) along a carbonate vein in a specimen of nickel ore from Thompson, Manitoba. Darker matrix is an intergrowth of acicular to granular millerite, pyrrhotite, chalcopyrite and violarite with a predominantly biotite, carbonate, and quartz gangue. F.O.V. ~8.8 cm x 11.0 cm. Specimen from INCO MB.

mil 2 Polished face showing acicular radial to massive millerite from Thompson Manitoba. Gangue is mostly carbonate. F.O.V. ~6.4 mm x 8.0 mm. Specimen from INCO MB.

mil 3 Photomicrograph showing a radial aggregate of acicular millerite crystals with light yellow to pale yellow-brown bireflectance. Polished thin section in plane polarized reflected light. F.O.V. ~0.34 mm x 0.43 mm.

mil 4 Photomicrograph showing the same field of view as in **mil 3**. Strong anisotropism varies from yellow to slate blue-grey. Polished thin section taken in cross polarized reflected light. F.O.V. ~0.34 mm x 0.43 mm.

Photographs submitted by P.J. Adamo and A.H. Mumin, Brandon University.

mil 1

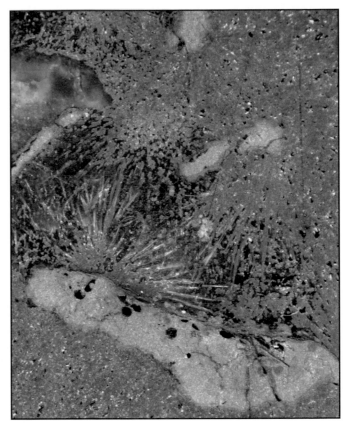

mil 2

mil 3

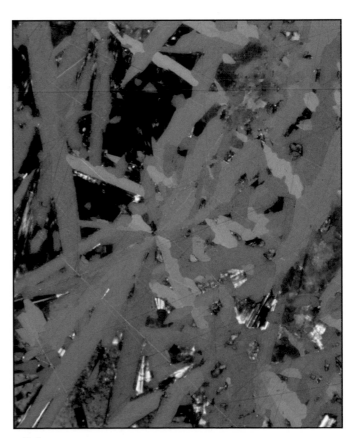

mil 4

Molybdenite (mo)

Environment: Porphyry, skarn, vein, magmatic, pegmatite

MoS_2

Trigonal

Characteristics

Hand Specimen	
Colour	Bluish grey to lead grey
Hardness	1 – 1½
Density	4.7 – 4.8

Polished Section			
Colour	White, pinkish tint	Cleavage	{0001} Perfect
Bireflectance	Very strong white to grey	Anisotropy	Very strong, pinkish white
Refl (546nm)	21.2 – 45.0	Refl (589nm)	20.5 – 44.2

Distinguishing Features

Lead grey colour with bluish tint, bluish grey streak, metallic lustre, perfect cleavage, and very soft greasy feel are characteristic in hand specimen. Molybdenite may be mistaken for graphite which has a dark grey streak, dull metallic lustre, and lower density. Molybdenite usually forms as tabular platy hexagonal crystals, and may also be massive or in small disseminated grains. In polished section, the softness (poor polish), bireflectance, and anisotropism are characteristic. Basal cleavage, straight extinction, and polysynthetic twinning are also typical. If polars are partly uncrossed, a characteristic dark blue colour is seen. Plates and flakes may be curved and show undulatory extinction. (N.B. The colour of molybdenite is darker in polished section than that of graphite, and graphite polarizes in yellowish rather than pinkish tints.)

Associated Minerals

Occurs in veins and disseminations with pyrite, chalcopyrite, bornite, cassiterite, wolframite, bismuthinite, and other sulphides.

Mode of Occurrence

Molybdenite is the most common molybdenum mineral. It occurs in disseminations and quartz veins with chalcopyrite, chalcocite, bornite, and sphalerite in some porphyry copper deposits and as the major economic mineral in porphyry molybdenite deposits such as Climax, Colorado, and Endako, British Columbia. It occurs as an accessory mineral in some granite and syenite and their associated pegmatite, and in mineralized pegmatite with cassiterite and wolframite. It also occurs in high-temperature molybdenite-scheelite-wolframite-topaz-fluorite veins, and vein-stockwork tin-tungsten deposits such as Mount Pleasant, New Brunswick . Molybdenite also occurs in some copper, copper-gold, and tungsten skarns.

References

Carten R.W., White W.H. and Stein H.J. (1993) High-grade granite-related molybdenum systems: Classification and origin. Geological Association of Canada, Special Paper 40, p. 521-554.

Maughan D.T., Keith J.D., Christiansen E.H., Pulsipher T., Hattori K. and Evans N.J. (2002) Contributions from mafic alkaline magmas to the Bingham porphyry Cu-Au-Mo deposit, Utah, USA. Mineralium Deposita, v. 37, p. 14-37.

van Leeuwen T. M., Taylor R., Coote A. and Longstaffe F.J. (1994) Porphyry molybdenum mineralization in a continental collision setting at Malala, Northwest Sulawesi, Indonesia. Journal of Geochemical Exploration, v. 50, p. 279-315.

White W.H., Bookstrom A.A., Kamilli R.J., Ganster M.W., Smith R.P., Ranta D.E. and Steininger R.C. (1981) Character and origin of the Climax-type molybdenum deposits. Economic Geology, 75th Anniversary Volume, p. 270-316.

Figures

mo 1   Molybdenite (grey) in quartz-feldspar matrix. Simon Fraser University collection. Photograph by Dan Marshall.

mo 2   Coarse molybdenite with pyrite in a late quartz stockwork veinlet, Pebble Copper (Cu-Au-Mo porphyry) deposit, southwestern Alaska. Molybdenite is paragenetically late and associated with quartz stockwork mineralization, particularly in the strong potassic altered core of the higher grade portion of the deposit. Submitted by Moira Smith, Teck Cominco.

mo 3   Molybdenite (mo) replaces chalcopyrite (cp) and chalcopyrite replaces pyrite (py). Pebble deposit, Alaska. Teck Cominco specimen 81:278. Reflected light.

mo 4   Lamellae of bireflectant molybdenite (mo) and needle like hematite (hem) with chalcopyrite (cp) rimmed by bornite (bn) and containing pyrite (py) inclusions. The gangue is tourmaline and siderite (sd). Guabisay, Ecuador. Teck Cominco specimen R92:14274. Photograph taken in plane polarized reflected light.

mo 1

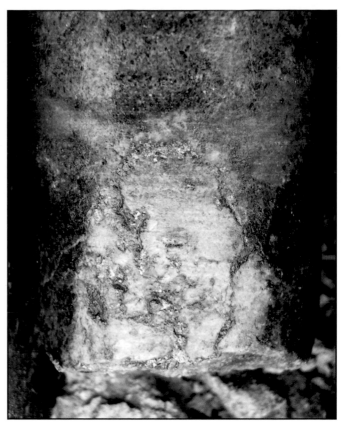

mo 2

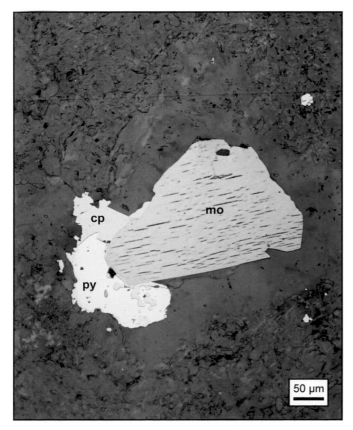

mo 3

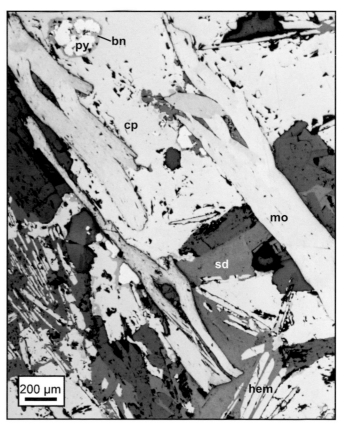

mo 4

Nickeline (nic)

Environment: Magmatic, vein, epithermal

NiAs

Hexagonal

Characteristics

Hand Specimen	
Colour	Pale copper-red, tarnishes grey-black
Hardness	5 – 5½
Density	7.8

Polished Section			
Colour	Yellowish, pink-brownish, pink	Cleavage	{1010}, {0001} Imperfect
Bireflectance	Strong; yellowish pink, violet pink, brownish pink	Anisotropy	Very strong, yellowish, greenish grey, violet blue, blue-grey
Refl (546nm)	48.1 – 52.2	Refl (589nm)	54.7 – 56.8

Distinguishing Features

The copper-red to pink colour, metallic lustre on fresh surfaces, dark brown to black streak, high density, and relatively high hardness are diagnostic for nickeline (*niccolite*) in hand specimen. It may develop a dark tarnish and, if heated, it may give off a garlic odour. In polished section, the colour, strong bireflectance, very strong anisotropism, good polish, and high reflectance are diagnostic. Pyrrhotite has lower reflectivity and is more yellow-brown than nickeline.

Associated Minerals

Commonly intergrown with Ni-Co-Fe arsenides, silver-bearing minerals, or with pyrrhotite and chalcopyrite.

Mode of Occurrence

Nickeline, with other nickel arsenide and sulphide, commonly occurs in, or associated with, norite. Also occurs in vein deposits with cobalt, copper, and silver minerals, for example at Cobalt, Ontario. Rarely forming crystals, it occurs as massive anhedral granular aggregates and reniform bands, or as complex intergrowths with other sulphide minerals.

References

Abzalov M.Z., Brewer T.S. and Polezhaeva L.I. (1997) Chemistry and distribution of accessory Ni, Co, Fe arsenic minerals in the Pechenga Ni-Cu deposits, Kola Peninsula, Russia. Mineralogy and Petrology. v. 61, p. 145-161.

Barrie C.T., Corfu F., Davis P., Coutts A.C. and MacEachern D. (1999) Geochemistry of the Dundonald komatiite-basalt suite and genesis of Dundeal Ni deposit, Abitibi Subprovince, Canada. Economic Geology, v. 94, p. 845-866.

Chen Y., Fleet M.E. and Pan Y. (1993) Platinum-group minerals and gold in arsenic-rich ore at the Thompson Mine, Thompson Nickel Belt, Manitoba, Canada. Mineralogy and Petrology, v. 49, p. 127-146.

Nesbitt H.W. and Reinke M. (1999) Properties of As and S at NiAs, NiS, and $F_{1-x}S$ surfaces, and reactivity of nickeline in air and water. American Mineralogist, v. 84, p. 639-649.

Wagner T. and Lorenz J. (2002) Mineralogy of complex Co-Ni-Bi vein mineralization, Bieber deposit, Spessart, Germany. Mineral Magazine, v. 66, p. 385-407.

Figures

nic 1 Nickeline (brassy) with quartz, biotite, minor chalcopyrite and secondary nickel oxides (green) from Thompson, Manitoba. F.O.V. ~4.7 cm x 5.9 cm. Specimen from INCO MB.

nic 2 Nickeline (brassy), cobalt-arsenides (grey), and secondary nickel oxides (green) from a vein deposit, Blanchet Island, Great Slave Lake, NWT. F.O.V. ~7.6 cm x 9.5 cm.

nic 3 Photomicrograph of a nickeline polycrystalline intergrowth illustrating the subtle range of bireflectance in plane polarized reflected light. Polished thin section. F.O.V. ~1.36 mm x 1.70 mm.

nic 4 Photomicrograph showing the same field of view as in **nic 3**, exhibiting more intense anisotropic colours in cross polarized reflected light. Polished thin section. F.O.V. ~1.36 mm x 1.70 mm.

Photographs submitted by P.J. Adamo and A.H. Mumin, Brandon University, Manitoba.

nic 1

nic 2

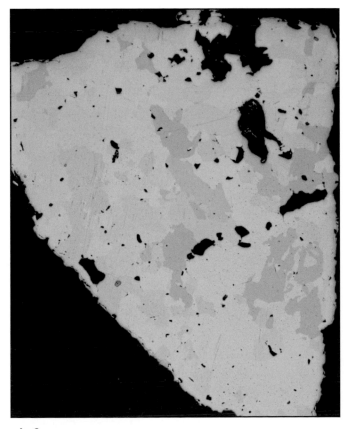

nic 3

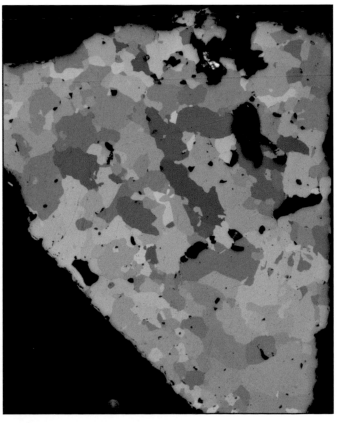

nic 4

Orpiment (orp)

Environment: Epithermal, hot spring

As_2S_3

Monoclinic

Characteristics

Hand Specimen	
Colour	Lemon yellow
Hardness	1½ – 2
Density	3.5

Polished Section			
Colour	Grey	Cleavage	{010} Perfect
Bireflectance	Strong, white, grey	Anisotropy	Strong but masked by internal reflections
Refl (546nm)	20.4 – 27.0	Refl (589nm)	19.6 – 26.2

Distinguishing Features

In hand specimen, orpiment is orange-yellow to yellow, with a resinous lustre on fresh surfaces, and pearly on cleavage faces. It is soft and has a pale yellow streak. In polished section, it has a grey colour and takes a difficult polish, often exhibiting scratches. Low reflectance, and strong anisotropism masked by even stronger light yellow internal reflections are diagnostic. Orpiment is generally associated with irregular plate-like masses of realgar. It usually occurs as radiating or anhedral masses, or as lath-like crystals, though crystals of orpiment are rare.

Associated Minerals

Orpiment is a rare mineral usually associated with realgar and formed under similar conditions. It also occurs with stibnite, arsenopyrite, arsenic, cinnabar, marcasite, pyrite, enargite, and sphalerite.

Mode of Occurrence

Orpiment is formed in low-temperature epithermal and hot spring environments, generally as a late-stage alteration mineral. It forms as deposits with realgar from geyser waters in the Norris Geyser Basin, Yellowstone National Park. It commonly occurs as thin alteration crusts on the edges of realgar. Orpiment is common in gold deposits of the Carlin Trend, Nevada.

References

Asadi H.H., Voncken J.H.L., Kuhnel R.A.and Hale M. (2000) Petrography, mineralogy and geochemistry of the Zarshuran Carlin-like gold deposit, northwest Iran. Mineralium Deposita, v. 35, p. 656-671.

Ferrini V., Martarelli L., De Vito C. and Deda T. (2003) The Koman dawsonite and realgar-orpiment deposit, northern Albania: Inferences on processes of formation. Canadian Mineralogist, v. 41, p. 413-427.

Groff J.A., Campbell A.R. and Norman D.I. (2002) An evaluation of fluid inclusion microthermometric data for orpiment-realgar-calcite-barite-gold mineralization at the Betze and Carlin mines, Nevada. Economic Geology, v. 97, p. 1341-1346.

Powell W.G. and Pattison D.R.M. (1997) An exsolution origin for low-temperature sulfides at the Hemlo gold deposit, Ontario, Canada. Economic Geology, v. 92, p. 569-577.

Figures

orp 1 Orpiment (yellow) with orange-reddish realgar from Manhattan, Nevada. F.O.V. ~6.5 cm x 8.2 cm.

orp 2 Massive crystalline orpiment from Nevada. F.O.V. ~2.9 cm x 3.6 cm.

orp 3 Photomicrograph of massive orpiment with minor realgar (upper right). Grey-white to whitish bireflectance is subtle in this photomicrograph. Polished thin section taken in plane polarized reflected light. F.O.V. ~0.68 mm x 0.85 mm.

orp 4 Photomicrograph of same area as **orp 3**. Strong greyish to yellow anisotropism in this specimen is only partly masked by brilliant internal reflections. Reddish area in upper part of photo is realgar. Polished thin section photograph taken under cross polarized reflected light. F.O.V. ~0.68 mm x 0.85 mm.

Photographs submitted by P.J. Adamo and A.H. Mumin, Brandon University.

orp 1

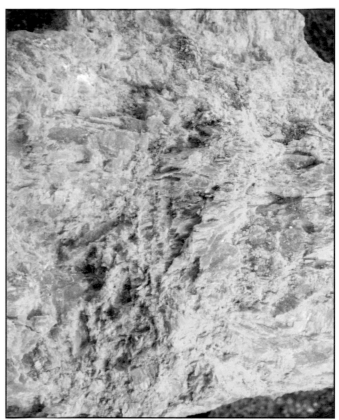

orp 2

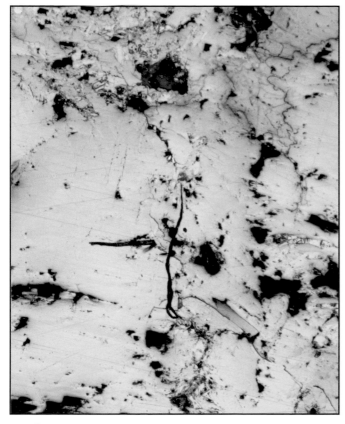

orp 3

orp 4

Pentlandite (pn)

Environment: Magmatic

$(Fe,Ni)_9S_8$

Cubic

Characteristics

Hand Specimen	
Colour	Yellowish bronze
Hardness	3½ – 4
Density	4.6 – 5.0

Polished Section			
Colour	Light cream to yellowish	Cleavage	{111} Parting
Bireflectance	None	Anisotropy	Isotropic
Refl (546nm)	49.5	Refl (589nm)	51.8

Distinguishing Features

Pentlandite is difficult to distinguish from pyrrhotite and pyrite in hand specimen. It is brassy yellow, metallic, with a brown streak, and high density. However, it is not magnetic and exhibits octahedral parting, unlike pyrrhotite. In polished section, the light cream to yellow colour and intimate association with pyrrhotite (as lamellae or exsolution flames) are characteristic. In addition, it takes a very good polish, has high reflectance, and is isotropic.

Associated Minerals

Pentlandite is the principal ore of nickel. Associated minerals include pyrrhotite, chalcopyrite, pyrite, violarite, millerite, cubanite, chromite, ilmenite, magnetite, and sperrylite.

Mode of Occurrence

Pentlandite is usually found in a massive habit and as flames and exsolutions intimately associated with pyrrhotite and chalcopyrite. It also occurs as granular veinlets and disseminated grains or aggregates. Major deposits include magmatic Ni-Cu ores at Sudbury, Ontario; Thompson, Manitoba; Voisey's Bay, Labrador; Kambalda, Western Australia; and Norilsk, Siberia. Cobaltian pentlandite is a common source of cobalt in IOCG deposits (e.g. Kuusamo schist belt deposits in Finland).

References

Craig, J.R. and Solberg T.N. (1999) Compositional zoning in ore minerals at the Craig mine, Sudbury, Ontario, Canada. Canadian Mineralogist, v. 37, p. 1163-1176.

Kelly D.P. and Vaughan D.J. (1983) Pyrrhotine-pentlandite ore textures: A mechanistic approach. Mineralogical Magazine, v. 47, p. 453-463.

Naldrett A.J., Singh J., Krstic S. and Li C.S. (2000) The mineralogy of the Voisey's Bay Ni-Cu-Co deposit, northern Labrador, Canada: Influence of oxidation state on textures and mineral compositions. Economic Geology, v. 95, p. 889-900.

Riley J.F. (1977) The pentlandite group $(Fe,Ni,Co)_9S_8$: New data and an appraisal of structure composition relationships. Mineralogical Magazine, v. 41, p. 345-349.

Vanhanen E. (2001) Geology, Mineralogy and Geochemistry of the Fe-Co-Au-(U) Deposits in the Paleoproterozoic Kuusamo Schist Belt, northeastern Finland. Geological Survey of Finland, Bulletin 399, 229 p.

Figures

pn 1   Drill core (left) and split and polished drill core (right) from Thompson, Manitoba, showing pentlandite aggregates or "eyes" (lighter) in a massive pyrrhotite matrix with graphite laths (dark). F.O.V. left 3.4 cm x 8.6 cm, and right 1.6 cm x 3.9 cm. Specimen from INCO MB. Photograph by P.J. Adamo, Brandon University.

pn 2   Polished slab showing pyrrhotite (brownish). Many of the silicate inclusions (black) hosted within the pyrrhotite are rimmed by pentlandite (whitish). Specimen also contains chalcopyrite and minor pyrite. Shebandowan deposit, Ontario. Submitted by D.H. Watkinson, Carleton University.

pn 3   Top: pentlandite eyes (light) in pyrrhotite (pinky beige) with graphite laths (medium grey) from Thompson (F.O.V. 0.68 mm x 0.51 mm.) Bottom: flame-like exsolution of pentlandite (lighter) in pyrrhotite (F.O.V. 0.14 mm x 0.07 mm). Photomicrograph taken under plane polarized reflected light. Submitted by P.J. Adamo and A.H. Mumin, Brandon University.

pn 4   Photomicrograph taken under plane polarized reflected light of pentlandite veinlets (light creamy) intergrown with pyrrhotite (pinky beige). Also present within pyrrhotite are rounded magnetite (grey) and minor yellow chalcopyrite. Rankin deposit, NWT. F.O.V. 0.68 mm x 0.85 mm. Submitted by P.J. Adamo and A.H. Mumin, Brandon University.

pn 1

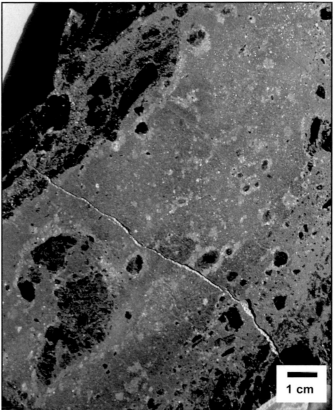

1 cm

pn 2

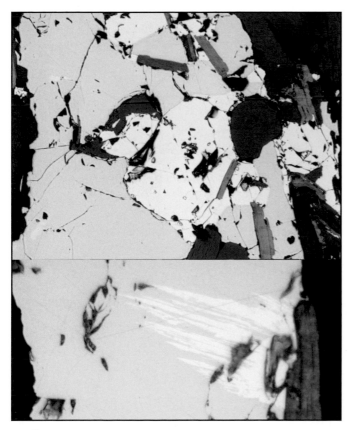

pn 3

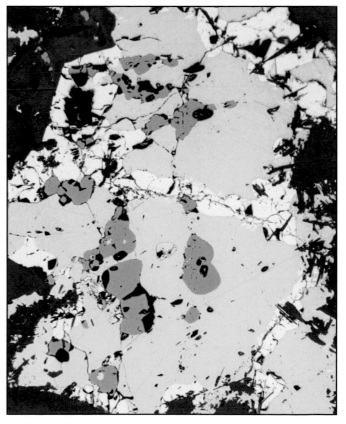

pn 4

Proustite–Pyrargyrite (pr-pyra)

Environment: Epithermal, vein

$Ag_3AsS_3 - Ag_3SbS_3$

Trigonal

Characteristics

Proustite (pr)

Hand Specimen		Polished Section			
Colour	Greyish with vermillion tint	**Colour**	Cinnabar-red, tarnishes black	**Cleavage**	{1011} Good
Hardness	2 – 2½	**Bireflectance**	Very weak to distinct; yellowish, blue-grey	**Anisotropy**	Strong
Density	5.6	**Refl (546nm)**	29.6 – 31.9	**Refl (589nm)**	27.9 – 30.0

Pyrargyrite (pyra)

Hand Specimen		Polished Section			
Colour	Reddish grey	**Colour**	Bluish grey	**Cleavage**	{1011} Distinct
Hardness	2 – 2½	**Bireflectance**	Very weak to distinct	**Anisotropy**	Strong, grey to dark grey
Density	5.9	**Refl (546nm)**	27.9 – 33.5	**Refl (589nm)**	26.0 – 31.4

Distinguishing Features

Proustite and pyrargyrite are closely related, isostructural minerals with similar compositions. Proustite is bright scarlet-red to reddish orange, adamantine, with a red streak, while pyrargyrite is a darker red to red-black, adamantine, with a cherry-red streak. Both are quite soft, and in crystalline form, both may be translucent, though proustite crystals may tend toward transparency, while pyrargyrite tends to be more opaque. Proustite and pyrargyrite can be reactive to light and darken upon exposure. In polished section, both are a bluish-grey colour, with pyrargyrite being somewhat darker than proustite. Both may rarely exhibit distinct bireflectance, low reflectance, strong anisotropy, striated faces, and very abundant red internal reflections, particularly in proustite.

Associated Minerals

Relatively rare minerals, they commonly occur as an alteration of native silver, and are routinely referred to as "ruby silver". They are associated with nickel-cobalt minerals and silver sulphosalts, galena, sphalerite, pyrite, carbonate minerals and quartz.

Mode of Occurrence

Proustite and pyrargyrite are generally low-temperature hydrothermal minerals found in vein and epithermal deposits, and are typically paragenetically late or secondary. Common in some high-grade, carbonate-hosted Ag deposits in Mexico (e.g. Zacatecas, Mexico). Also found in deposits in Cobalt, Ontario; Atacama, Chile; and San Cristobal, Bolivia. Proustite is the less common of the two minerals, and is usually found with pyrargyrite, and in more arsenic-rich environments.

References

Kracek F.C. (1946) Phase relations in the system silver-sulfur and the transitions in silver sulfide. Transactions of the American Geophysical Union, v. 27, p. 367-74.

Petruk W. (1975) Mineralogy and geology of the Zgounder silver deposit in Morocco. Canadian Mineralogist, v. 13, p. 43-54.

Petruk W. and staff (1971) Characteristics of the sulphides. Canadian Mineralogist, v. 11, p. 196-231.

Figures

pr 1 Proustite, O'Brien deposit, Cobalt Ontario. Specimen LT240 from Lloyd Twaites.

pr 2 Proustite crystals with pyrargyrite, quartz, chalcopyrite and galena. Proustite displays reddish internal reflections. Uchuchacua deposit, Huanuco Department, Perú. Specimen S98.37 from Art Soregaroli.

pr 3 Pyrargyrite (pyra) with minor pyrite (py) in a vug from the Reyes mine in Mexico. Note the abundant scratches and minor reddish internal reflections. Photograph taken in plane polarized reflected light. Sample provided by Roger Poulin.

pr 4 Corresponding photograph under partly crossed polars showing the strong anistropism in pyrargyrite, abundant red internal reflections, and striated faces (arrows). Striated faces are exhibited in reflected light, but are more pronounced in transmitted light (see inset of arrowed grain).

Photographs by Dan Marshall.

pr 1

pr 2

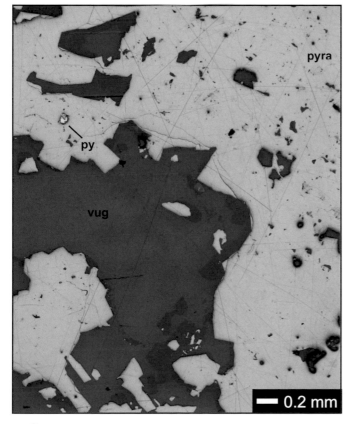

pr 3

pr 4

Pyrite (py)

Environment: All environments

FeS_2

Cubic

Characteristics

Hand Specimen	
Colour	Brassy yellow
Hardness	6 – 6½
Density	5.0 – 5.2

Polished Section			
Colour	Yellowish white	Cleavage	{001} Poor
Bireflectance	Not present	Anisotropy	Weak
Refl (546nm)	54.1	Refl (589nm)	55.2

Distinguishing Features

Pyrite is a brassy yellowish colour with a metallic lustre and commonly striated faces on cubic, pyritohedral, and octahedral crystals. Pyrite can be confused with chalcopyrite and pyrrhotite. The fresh surface of pyrite is generally less yellow than chalcopyrite, and pyrrhotite generally displays a pinkish hue and may be magnetic. Pyrite is also known as "fools gold", but can be distinguished from gold by its hardness, greenish black streak, and density. In polished section, pyrite is yellowish white, lighter than chalcopyrite, has high reflectance, displays no bireflectance, and is usually isotropic but sometimes displays anomalous weak anisotropy.

Associated Minerals

It can be found associated with practically all common minerals and in most ore deposit types, but occurs most frequently with chalcopyrite, sphalerite, galena, arsenopyrite, and pyrrhotite.

Mode of Occurrence

Pyrite is the most common and widespread of the sulphide minerals. It is almost ubiquitous in Au, VMS, and porphyry deposits. It occurs as euhedral cubes and pyritohedra, anhedral crystalline masses, and colloform bands of very fine grains. Growth zoning may be visible. It forms at both high and low temperatures and occurs in hydrothermal veins, sedimentary, igneous, and metamorphic rocks. Almost never mined as an ore of Fe, pyrite has at times been important as a significant source of sulphur.

References

Brooker D.D., Craig J.R. and Rimstidt J.D. (1987) Ore metamorphism and pyrite porphyroblast development at the Cherokee Mine, Ducktown, Tennessee. Economic Geology, v. 82, p. 72-86.

Craig J.R., Vokes F.M. and Solberg T.N. (1998) Pyrite; physical and chemical textures. Mineralium Deposita, v. 34, p. 82-101.

England B.M. and Ostwald J. (1993) Framboid-derived structures in some Tasman fold belt base-metal sulphide deposits, New South Wales, Australia. Ore Geology Reviews, v. 7, p. 381-412.

Foley N., Ayuso R.A. and Seal R.R. (2001) Remnant colloform pyrite at the Haile gold deposit, South Carolina: A textural key to genesis. Economic Geology, v. 96, p. 891-902.

Simon G., Kesler S.E. and Chryssoulis S. (1999) Geochemistry and textures of gold bearing arsenian pyrite, Twin Creeks, Nevada: Implications for deposition of gold in Carlin-type deposits. Economic Geology, v. 94, p. 405-421.

Figures

py 1   Fine-grained basal pyritic zone enveloped by moderately recrystallized pyrite-sphalerite-galena with weak layering and secondary milky quartz pods and veins, 850 metre level, Brunswick No. 12 Zn-Pb-Cu-Ag deposit, Bathurst, New Brunswick. Submitted by Dave Lentz, University of New Brunswick.

py 2   Pyrite in Archean banded iron formation from the Carshaw property, southeast of TImmins, Ontario. The specimen shows alternating bands of coarse white quartz and brassy, tarnished pyrite, the latter in crystals as large as 6 to 15 mm. The pyrite has a porous internal texture, with carbonate the predominant void-filling mineral. The ore also contains minor chlorite on pyrite grain boundaries and native gold in fractures within the sulphide. Submitted by Graham Wilson, Turnstone Geological Ltd.

py 3   Pyrite (py) in a tertiary sulphide-carbonate vein from the Hardy showing, Sudbury, ON. The pyrite is shown in contact with galena (gn), sphalerite (sph), and chalcopyrite (cp). Simon Fraser University collection. Plane polarized reflected light. Photograph by Dan Marshall.

py 4   Pyrite with gold inclusion, in contact with tetradymite, gold and quartz. Beaufor deposit, Quebec. F.O.V. 2.5 mm. Submitted by Jonathan Roussy.

py 1

py 2

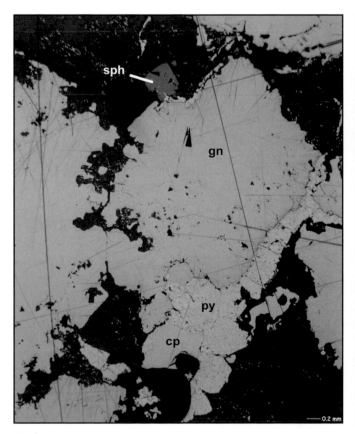

py 3

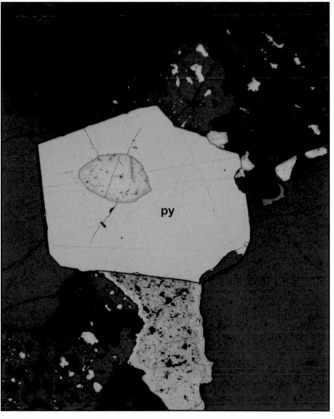

py 4

Pyrochlore (pycl)

Environment: Pegmatite, carbonatite

$(Na,Ca)_2(Nb,Ti,Ta)_2O_6(OH,F,O)$

Cubic

Characteristics

Hand Specimen	
Colour	Brown, greenish, reddish
Hardness	5 – 5½
Density	4.2 – 6.4

Polished Section			
Colour	Grey	Cleavage	Indistinct
Bireflectance	Not seen	Anisotropy	Isotropic
Refl (546nm)	10.5	Refl (589nm)	10.6

Distinguishing Features

Pyrochlore is dark reddish to blackish brown, with a yellowish brown streak, resinous to vitreous to greasy lustre, brittle, with a conchoidal fracture, and an octahedral form when crystalline. In polished section, it has a grey colour, good polish, low reflectance (less than magnetite and sphalerite), is isotropic, and exhibits brownish to yellowish internal reflections. It generally forms euhedral to subhedral crystals, which may be zoned. Pyrochlore may incorporate some U or Th into its structure and may then exhibit some radioactivity.

Associated Minerals

Niobo-tantalate minerals (including columbite, and tantalite), apatite, allanite, zircon, carbonate minerals, nepheline, ilmenite, cassiterite, rutile, and biotite.

Mode of Occurrence

Pyrochlore is a relatively rare mineral, however it is important as an ore of tantalum and niobium. Pyrochlore is the Nb-rich end member of a solid solution series with microlite (Ta-rich end member). Pyrochlore is associated with carbonatite and nepheline syenite, while the more common microlite occurs in granitic pegmatite dykes and rarely in carbonatite. Pyrochlore is found at Oka, Quebec; Strange Lake, Labrador-Quebec border; and Thor Lake, NWT. Generally has a granular habit, as anhedral to subhedral crystals disseminated in matrix. Also, forms octahedral crystals that may be twinned.

References

Chakhmouradian A.R. and Sitnikova M.A. (1999) Radioactive minerals from murmanite-lorenzenite tinguaite at Mt. Selsurt, Lovozero Complex, Kola Peninsula. European Journal of Mineralogy, v. 11, p. 871-878.

Lumpkin G.R. and Ewing R.C (1992) Geochemical alteration of pyrochlore group minerals: Microlite subgroup. American Mineralogist, v. 77, p. 179-187.

Lumpkin G.R. and Ewing R.C. (1995) Geochemical alteration of pyrochlore group minerals; pyrochlore subgroup. American Mineralogist, v. 80, p. 732-743.

Richardson D.G. and Birkett T.C. (1996) Peralkaline rock-associated rare metals. in Geology of Canadian Mineral Deposit Types, (ed.) O.R. Eckstrand, W.D. Sinclair and R.I. Thorpe. Geological Survey of Canada, Geology of Canada No. 8, p. 523-540.

Richardson D.G. and Birkett T.C. (1996) Carbonatite-associated deposits in Geology of Canadian Mineral Deposit Types, (ed.) O.R. Eckstrand, W.D. Sinclair, and R.I. Thorpe. Geological Survey of Canada, Geology of Canada No. 8, p. 541-558.

Tindle A.G. and Breaks F.W. (1998) Oxide minerals of the Separation Rapids rare-element granitic pegmatite group, northwestern Ontario. Canadian Mineralogist, v. 36, p. 609-635.

Figures

pycl 1 Pyrochlore in carbonate matrix. Verity property, Blue River, British Columbia. Scale: each square = 1 cm. Specimen from Tom Schroeter.

pycl 2 Pyrochlore in carbonatite matrix. Verity property, Blue River, British Columbia. Specimen LT953 from Lloyd Twaites.

pycl 3 Pyrochlore (pycl) and latrappite (ltr) in carbonatite matrix. Oka Carbonatite Complex, Quebec. Plane polarized transmitted light. Specimen from David H. Watkinson, Carleton University.

pycl 4 Corresponding photomicrograph in plane polarized reflected light.

Photographs by Dan Marshall.

pycl 1

pycl 2

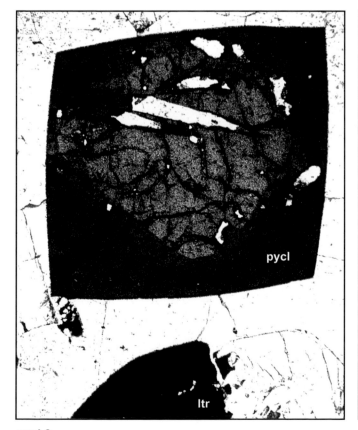

pycl 3

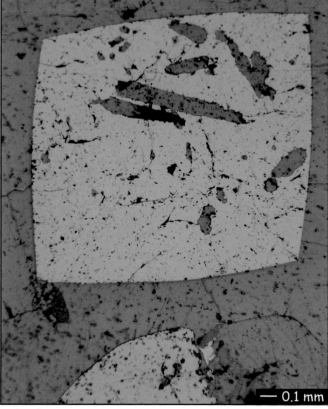

pycl 4

Pyrolusite (pyl)

Environment: Secondary, hydrothermal, sedimentary

MnO_2

Tetragonal

Characteristics

Hand Specimen	
Colour	Iron black
Hardness	$2 - 6\frac{1}{2}$
Density	$4.4 - 5.1$

Polished Section			
Colour	Creamy white	Cleavage	{110} Perfect
Bireflectance	Distinct in oil, yellowish white to grey-white	Anisotropy	Very strong, yellowish, brownish, blue
Refl (546nm)	$18.7 - 31.3$	Refl (589nm)	$18.4 - 30.4$

Distinguishing Features

In hand specimen, pyrolusite is black to grey-black, may have a bluish tint, has dull to earthy lustre, and has a black to bluish black streak. The hardness can be quite variable depending on the habit, however in its common earthy form it is quite soft, often leaving a black residue on the fingers when handled. Dendritic shapes and nodules (pseudomorphs after manganite) are characteristic for pyrolusite. In polished section, it is white with a creamy yellow bireflectance and strong anisotropism.

Associated Minerals

Pyrolusite is the most common manganese mineral and an important ore of Mn. It is associated with all of the manganese oxide minerals, particularly psilomelane and manganite, and is also found with vanadinite, goethite, hematite, magnetite, and Fe-hydroxides.

Mode of Occurrence

Manganese is present in small amounts in most crystalline rocks. Manganese dissolved from these rock, may be redeposited as various minerals, primarily as pyrolusite. Pyrolusite may also be formed from the alteration of rhodochrosite ($MnCO_3$). Nodular deposits of pyrolusite occur in bogs, on lake bottoms, and on the ocean floor. Pyrolusite also occurs in veins with quartz and various metallic minerals. The major economic sources of manganese are sedimentary in origin and consist of carbonate and oxide minerals deposited as chemical sediments (e.g. Kalahari, South Africa). Supergene deposits are also an important source of manganese and consist of manganese oxide and hydroxide accumulations on deeply weathered manganese-rich rocks.

References

Burns R.G. and Burns V.M. (1979) Manganese oxides. Marine Minerals, v. 6, p. 1-46.

Gutzmer J. and Beukes N.J. (1996) Mineral paragenesis of the Kalahari manganese field, South Africa. Ore Geology Reviews, v. 11, p. 405-428.

Miura H. and Hariya Y. (1997) Manganese mineralization; geochemistry and mineralogy of terrestrial and marine deposits. Geological Society Special Publication 119, p. 281-299.

Oyman T., Minareci F. and Piskin Ö. (2003) Efemçukuru B-rich epithermal gold deposit (Zmir, Turkey). Ore Geology Reviews, v. 23, p. 35-53.

Staudhammer K.P. and Murr L.E. (1974) Characterization of natural pyrolusite by electron microscopy. Contributions to Mineralogy and Petrology, v. 45, p. 251-256.

Figures

pyl 1 "Ropey" textured pyrolusite (grey) with hexagonal orange-brown vanadinite crystals, Taouz, Morocco. Specimen S85.47 from Art Soregaroli. Photograph by Dan Marshall.

pyl 2 Photomicrograph of massive pyrolusite (location unknown). Bireflectance is well displayed in upper and middle part of aggregate. Plane reflected light. F.O.V. 1.4 mm x 1.7 mm. Submitted by C.G. Couëslan and A.H. Mumin, Brandon University, Manitoba.

pyl 3 Photomicrograph of **pyl 2** displaying strong anisotropism. Reflected light with crossed polars.

pyl 1

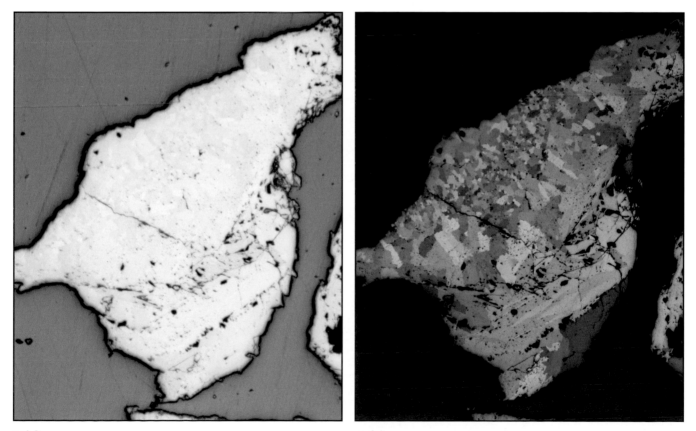

pyl 2

pyl 3

Pyrrhotite (po)

Environment: Magmatic, skarn, SEDEX, VMS mesothermal

$Fe_{1-x}S$

Hexagonal, Monoclinic

Characteristics

Hand Specimen	
Colour	Bronzy yellow
Hardness	3½ – 4½
Density	4.5 – 4.8

Polished Section			
Colour	Yellow, pinkish hues	Cleavage	{0001}, {1120} Imperfect
Bireflectance	Very distinct, creamy brown to reddish brown	Anisotropy	Very strong, red to yellowish brown
Refl (546nm)	34.8 – 37.4	Refl (589nm)	37.0 – 39.7

Distinguishing Features

Variably magnetic, pyrrhotite is a bronzy yellow-brown colour, with a grey-black streak, and a metallic lustre, but tarnishes quickly. It is often difficult to distinguish from chalcopyrite, pyrite, marcasite, and pentlandite, but none of these minerals are magnetic. In polished section, it is a pale pink-brown to creamy brown with distinct bireflectance, strong anisotropism (except in basal section), and often exhibits basal cleavage. Pyrrhotite has two crystal structures, the hexagonal variety is usually slightly darker than monoclinic pyrrhotite. The stoichiometric end member (troilite: FeS) is non magnetic. The higher temperature, hexagonal form of pyrrhotite is closer to stoichiometric and less magnetic than the lower temperature, monoclinic (less stoichiometric) form.

Associated Minerals

Occurs with most other common sulphides, such as chalcopyrite, pentlandite, marcasite, arsenopyrite, and pyrite. In Ni-ores, exsolved lamellae and "flames" of pentlandite are common in pyrrhotite.

Mode of Occurrence

Pyrrhotite is commonly associated with basic igneous rocks (for example in the Bushveld layered intrusion), particularly norites. It occurs as disseminated grains or, as at Sudbury, Ontario, as large masses in magmatic nickel deposits associated with pentlandite, chalcopyrite, or other sulphides. Pyrrhotite is a major constituent of VMS deposits and is also found in skarn deposits, high-temperature vein deposits, and pegmatites.

References

Durazzo A. and Taylor L.A. (1982) Exsolution in the Mss-pentlandite system; textural and genetic implications for Ni-sulfide ores. Mineralium Deposita, v. 17, p. 313-332.

Kelly D.P. and Vaughan D.J. (1983) Pyrrhotite-pentlandite ore textures: A mechanistic approach. Mineralogical Magazine v. 47, p. 453-463.

Li C., Naldrett A.J., Rucklidge J.C. and Kilius L.R. (1993) Concentrations of platinum-group elements and gold in sulfides from the Strathcona Deposit, Sudbury, Ontario. Canadian Mineralogist, v. 31, p. 523-531.

O'Reilly W., Hoffmann V., Chouker A.C., Soffel H.C. and Menyeh A. (2000) Magnetic properties of synthetic analogues of pyrrhotite ore in the grain size range 1-24 μm. Geophysical Journal International, v. 142, p. 669-683.

Zhou T., Phillips G.N., Dong G. and Myers R.E. (1995) Pyrrhotite in the Witwatersrand gold fields, South Africa. Economic Geology, v. 90, p. 2361-2369.

Figures

po 1 Massive pyrrhotite. Simon Fraser University collection. Edge of coin is 1.9 cm. Photograph by Holly Keyes.

po 2 Hand specimen of massive sulphide ore from Oktyabrysk deposit, Kharealkh Intrusion, Noril'sk Region. Pyrrhotite (po) occurs as discrete crystals surrounded by loops of chalcopyrite (cp) and granular pentlandite (pn). The ore type is often termed "loop texture sulphide". Photograph by Peter Lightfoot, INCO.

po 3 Pyrrhotite (pinkish grey) with poikilitic amphibole (dark grey). Photomicrograph taken in plane- polarized reflected light. Specimen from the Simon Fraser University collection. Photograph by Dan Marshall.

po 4 Corresponding photomicrograph under partly crossed polars, showing the characteristic red to brown anisotropic colours of pyrrhotite.

po 1

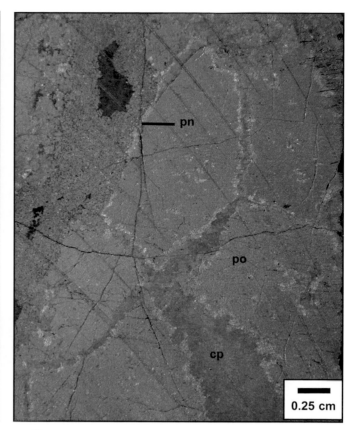

po 2

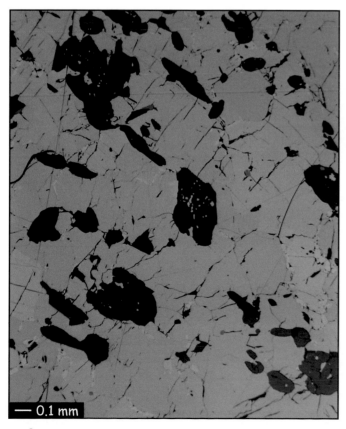

po 3

po 4

Realgar (rea)

Environment: Epithermal, hot spring

AsS

Monoclinic

Characteristics

Hand Specimen	
Colour	Red to orange
Hardness	1½ – 2
Density	3.5 – 3.6

Polished Section			
Colour	Dull grey	Cleavage	{010} Good
Bireflectance	Weak but distinct; grey with reddish to bluish tint	Anisotropy	Moderate to strong; masked by internal reflections
Refl (546nm)	19.9	Refl (589nm)	19.3

Distinguishing Features

In hand specimen, realgar is a distinctive orange to red colour, with an orange to orange-yellow streak, a resinous to sub-metallic lustre, and is very soft. Crystals are translucent to transparent, and realgar disintegrates slowly on exposure to light, eventually to a powder. In polished section, it is a dull grey colour, with weak bireflectance, and strong anisotropism masked by abundant and intense yellowish red internal reflections. It takes a poor polish, evidenced by abundant scratches. Association with orpiment is characteristic for realgar. Some specimens of realgar fluoresce and it may give off a garlic odour upon heating.

Associated Minerals

Realgar is associated with orpiment, cinnabar, graphite, pyrite, sphalerite, arsenopyrite, arsenic, arsenic-sulphosalts (e.g. tennantite and proustite), and stibnite. Also occurs with ores of silver and gold.

Mode of Occurrence

Realgar occurs in veins and replacement deposits of lead, silver, and gold ores. It also occurs as a volcanic sublimation product and as deposits associated with hot springs. It is deposited from geyser waters in the Norris Geyser Basin, Yellowstone National Park. Other localities include Almaden, Spain; Carlin Trend, Nevada; and Hemlo gold deposits, Ontario.

References

Ferrini V., Martarelli L., De Vito C., Cina A. and Deda T. (2003) The Koman dawsonite and realgar-orpiment deposit, north-ern Albania: Inferences on processes of formation. Canadian Mineralogist, v. 41, p. 413-427.

Groff J.A., Campbell A.R. and Norman D.I. (2002) An evaluation of fluid inclusion microthermometric data for orpiment-realgar-calcite-barite-gold mineralization at the Betze and Carlin mines, Nevada. Economic Geology, v. 97, p. 1341-1346.

Marquez-Zavalia F., Craig J.R. and Solberg T.N. (1999) Duranusite, product of realgar alteration, Mina Capitalis, Argentina, Canadian Mineralogist, v. 37, p. 1255-1259.

Xiong X.X. (2000) Classification, minerogenic models and prospecting of realgar/orpiment deposits in China. Acta Geologica Sinica, v. 74, p. 618-622.

Figures

rea 1   Massive crystalline realgar with traces of yellow orpiment from Nevada, USA. F.O.V. ~1.8 cm x 2.3 cm.

rea 2   Realgar intergrown with bladed yellow orpiment, Nevada, USA. F.O.V. ~2.9 cm x 3.6 cm.

rea 3   Photomicrograph of grey-white realgar with reddish orange internal reflections. Polished thin section in plane polarized reflected light. F.O.V. ~0.34 mm x 0.43 mm.

rea 4   Photomicrograph showing the same field of view as in **rea 3**, but taken in cross polarized reflected light. Intense orange-red internal reflections completely mask anisotropism. Polished thin section. F.O.V. ~0.34 mm x 0.43 mm.

Photographs submitted by A.H. Mumin and P.J. Adamo, Brandon University.

rea 1

rea 2

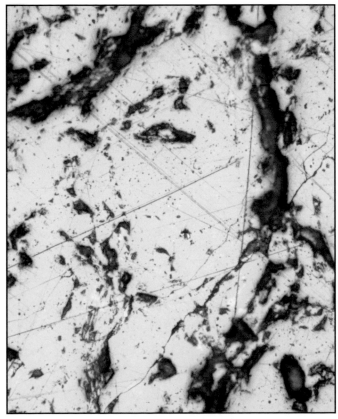

rea 3

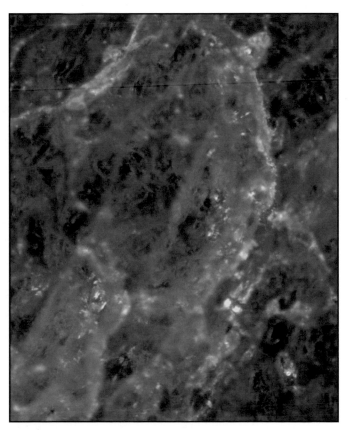

rea 4

Scheelite (sch)

Environment: Skarn, mesothermal, vein

$CaWO_4$

Tetragonal

Characteristics

Hand Specimen	
Colour	Grey - white
Hardness	4½ – 5
Density	5.9 – 6.1

Polished Section			
Colour	White, yellow, brown, greenish	Cleavage	Distinct {010}
Bireflectance	Not observed	Anisotropy	Masked by internal reflections
Refl (546nm)	11.6	Refl (589nm)	11.4

Distinguishing Features

Scheelite is distinguished by bluish white (to yellowish orange) fluorescence under shortwave ultraviolet light. In hand specimen, it can be colourless, white, yellow, orange, or brown and translucent to transparent. Streak is white, lustre is commonly vitreous to resinous, and density is high for a translucent mineral. In polished section, scheelite can be distinguished by its good polish, low reflectance (though high for a transparent mineral), and abundant white internal reflections. In thin section, scheelite is colourless to grey-brown, has very high relief and low birefringence.

Associated Minerals

Found with calc-silicate minerals (carbonate, garnet, diopside, and amphibole) in skarn deposits and with wolframite, arsenopyrite, pyrrhotite, bismuthinite, native bismuth, molybdenite, fluorite, tourmaline, and gold in intrusion-related and hydrothermal-vein deposits. Scheelite forms a series with powellite in which molybdenum substitutes for tungsten. Powellite fluoresces a yellow colour.

Mode of Occurrence

An important ore of tungsten (second to wolframite), scheelite commonly occurs in granular disseminated form in skarn deposits or as dipyramidal crystals and/or granular aggregates in pegmatite and veins. Scheelite is a common gangue mineral in some mesothermal gold-quartz-carbonate veins (e.g. Hollinger deposit, Ontario).

References

Anglin C.D., Franklin J.M. and Jonasson I.R. (1996) Sm-Nd dating of scheelite and tourmaline: Implications for the genesis of Archean gold deposits, Val d'Or, Canada. Economic Geology, v. 91, p. 1372-1382.

Brugger J., Maas R., Lahaye Y., McRae C., Ghaderi M., Costa S., Lambert D., Bateman R. and Prince K. (2002) Origins of Nd-Sr-Pb isotopic variations in single scheelite grains from Archaean gold deposits, Western Australia. Chemical Geology, v. 182, p. 203-225.

Kempe U., Belyatsk B.V., Krymsky R.S., Kremenetsky A.A. and Ivanov P.A. (2001) Sm-Nd and Sr isotope systematics of scheelite from the giant Au(-W) deposit Muruntau (Uzbekistan); Implications for the age and sources of Au mineralization. Mineralium Deposita, v. 36, p. 379-392.

Miguel G.L. and Inverno C.M.C. (2000) Mineralogy and metasomatic evolution of distal strata-bound scheelite skarns in the Riba de Alva Mine, Northeastern Portugal. Economic Geology, v. 95, p. 1259-1275.

Voicu G., Bardoux M., Stevenson R. and Jebrak M. (2000) Nd and Sr isotope study of hydrothermal scheelite and host rocks at Omai, Guiana Shield; implications for ore fluid source and flow path during the formation of orogenic gold deposits. Mineralium Deposita, v. 35, p. 302-314.

Figures

sch 1 Large crystals of brownish orange scheelite growing at vein margin of tourmalinized wall rock, and surrounded by tourmaline-rich vein material, grading into quartz. 1708W flat vein, Sigma Mine, Val d'Or, Quebec. Specimen and photograph by C.D. Anglin.

sch 2 Granular aggregates of crystalline scheelite in quartz-tourmaline vein, Hollinger Mine, Timmins Ontario. Gold is hosted in late fractures cutting the quartz (qtz), tourmaline (tur), and scheelite (sch). Specimen from C.D. Anglin, photograph width is 2.5 cm.

sch 3 Transmitted light photomicrograph of scheelite associated with tourmaline (tur), carbonate (twinned) and quartz (qtz) in gold-bearing vein in Pascalis Mine, Val d'Or, Quebec. Specimen 86-AAA-037 from C.D. Anglin.

sch 4 Same field of view as **sch 3** in crossed polars. Photograph by Dan Marshall.

sch 1

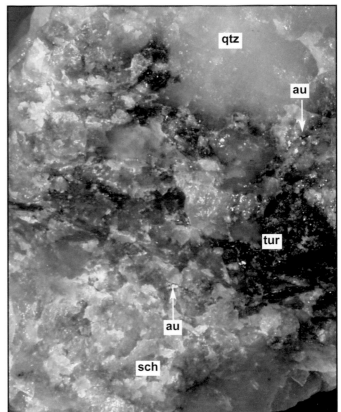

sch 2

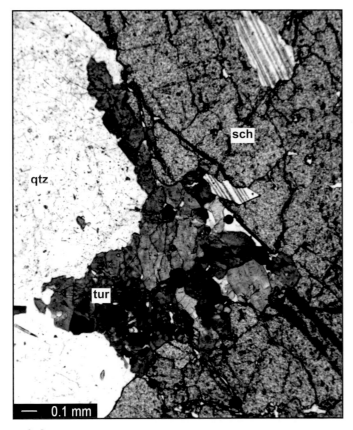

sch 3

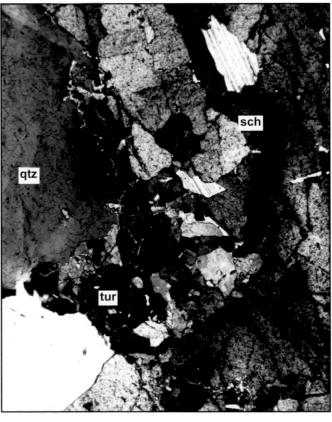

sch 4

Silver (ag)

Environment: Epithermal, vein

Ag

Cubic

Characteristics

Hand Specimen	
Colour	Silver white
Hardness	2.5 – 3
Density	10.5 (pure)

Polished Section			
Colour	Bright white with creamy tint, tarnishes easily	Cleavage	Absent
Bireflectance	Not present	Anisotropy	Isotropic
Refl (546nm)	81.0	Refl (589nm)	82.8

Distinguishing Features

The colour on fresh surfaces and streak of native silver are both silver-white. The high density, softness, ductility and malleability, hackley fracture, and black (acanthite) tarnish, are also characteristic. Crystals are rare, silver is more commonly found in silvery wires, dendritic masses, or flattened plates in hand specimen. In polished section, extremely high reflectivity and isotropism are distinctive. However, it characteristically appears falsely anisotropic due to the numerous scratches developed during polishing.

Associated Minerals

Native silver is commonly found associated with other silver sulphides (e.g. acanthite), silver minerals (e.g. pyrargyrite and proustite) Ni-Co-As minerals, and with other sulphides such as arsenopyrite, galena, sphalerite, and tetrahedrite-tennantite. Native silver commonly occurs in the five-element (Ni-Co-As-Ag-Bi) association and these deposits may also contain reserves of uranium.

Mode of Occurrence

Native silver is rare, though widely distributed in small amounts. Its most common occurrence is in hydrothermal veins such as those at Cobalt, Ontario; Great Bear Lake, NWT; and at Kongsberg, Norway. Native silver is also found in some epithermal deposits such as at Zacatecas, Mexico.

References

Kissin S.A. (1992) Five-element (Ni-Co-As-Ag-Bi) veins. Geoscience Canada, v. 19, p. 113-124.

Knight J. and Leitch C.H.B. (2001) Phase relations in the system Au-Cu-Ag at low temperatures, based on natural assemblages. Canadian Mineralogist, v. 39, p. 889-905.

Moller S.A., Islas F., Jorge E., Davila F. and Ramon T. (2001) New discoveries in the La Colorada district, Zacatecas state, Mexico. in New Mines and Discoveries in Mexico and Central America. Society of Economic Geologists, Special Publication No. 8, p. 95-104.

Petruk W., Harris D.C., Cabri L.J. and Stewart J.M. (1971) Characteristics of the silver-antimony minerals. Canadian Mineralogist, v. 12, p. 187-195.

Raines E. (1992) The geology, mineralogy, and history of four native silver localities in Colorado. Rocks and Minerals, v. 67, p. 230-254.

Sherlock R.L., Roth T., Spooner E.T.C. and Bray C.J. (1999) Origin of the Eskay Creek precious metal-rich volcanogenic massive sulfide deposit; fluid inclusion and stable isotope evidence. Economic Geology, v. 94, p. 803-824.

Figures

ag 1   Leaf and dendritic silver in quartz-sphalerite vein from Silver Mountain, Lybster Township, Thunder Bay District, Ontario. Coin diameter is 1.9 cm. Specimen number GSC4911 from I.R. Jonasson, Geological Survey of Canada.

ag 2   Slightly tarnished wire silver with black acanthite after argentite (arrow) and minor pyrite. Specimen 5141, from the Highland Bell deposit, Beaverdell, British Columbia. Submitted by Ross Beaty, Pan-American Silver.

ag 3   Silver (ag), nickeline and minor safflorite in carbonate gangue. Right of Way deposit, Cobalt Ontario. Plane polarized reflected light. Specimen from I.R. Jonasson, Geological Survey of Canada.

ag 4   Diagnostic scratches in silver and the corresponding anisotropy in nickeline (nic). Partially uncrossed polarized reflected light.

Photographs by Dan Marshall.

ag 1

ag 2

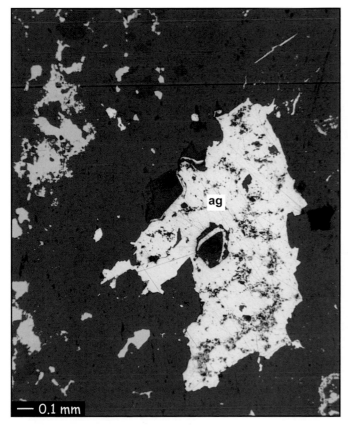

ag 3

ag 4

Sperrylite (spy)

Environment: Magmatic, pegmatite, placer

PtAs$_2$

Cubic

Characteristics

Hand Specimen	
Colour	Metallic white
Hardness	6 – 7
Density	10.6

Polished Section			
Colour	White	**Cleavage**	{001} Indistinct
Bireflectance	Not seen	**Anisotropy**	Isotropic
Refl (546nm)	55.2	**Refl (589nm)**	55.1

Distinguishing Features

Sperrylite is a tin-white colour in hand specimen, with a metallic lustre, black streak, and high specific gravity, and is characterized by the tendency to develop idiomorphically. It has a similar structure and crystal habit to pyrite, but is distinguished by its colour and hardness, which is relatively hard for metallic minerals. Cubic forms are commonly perfect and partly preserved in alluvial deposits. In polished section, the white colour, high reflectance, isotropism, and idiomorphic habit are diagnostic.

Associated Minerals

Usually associated with platinum and platinum group minerals (PGE), gold, pentlandite, pyrrhotite, pyrite, and chromite.

Mode of Occurrence

Sperrylite is a relatively rare mineral, but economically significant as an important ore of platinum, second to native platinum in importance. It occurs in basic pegmatite and is preserved in alluvial deposits. Most importantly it occurs in magmatic sulphide ores (e.g. Sudbury, Ontario), and in layered mafic intrusions (e.g. Stillwater, Montana and Bushveld, South Africa).

References

Barkov A.Y, Laflamme J.H.G., Cabri L.J. and Martin R.F. (2002) Platinum-group minerals from the Wellgreen Cu-Ni-PGE deposit, Yukon, Canada. Canadian Mineralogist, v. 40, p. 651-670.

Watkinson D.H. (1999) Platinum-group-element enrichment in Cu-Ni-rich sulfides from footwall deposits, Sudbury Igneous Complex, Canada. Chronique de la Recherche Miniere, v. 535, p. 29-43.

Weiner, K.L. and Hochleitner R. (1990) Mineral data for sperrylite PtAs$_2$: Translated from: Steckbrief; Sperrylith PtAs$_2$. Mineralien-Magazin, Lapis 15, p. 7-11.

Zaccarini F., Garuti G. and Cawthorn R.G. (2002) Platinum group minerals in chromitite xenoliths from the Onverwacht and Tweefontein ultramafic pipes, Eastern Bushveld Complex, South Africa. Canadian Mineralogist, v. 40, p. 481-497.

Figures

spy 1 Sperrylite crystals in chalcopyrite-rich matrix. Vermilion deposit, Denison Township, Sudbury district, Ontario. Size of largest crystal is 1 cm. ROM specimen M31065. Photograph by Bob Ramik, Royal Ontario Museum.

spy 2 Photomicrograph in reflected light of sperrylite (Spy: white), adjacent to telluride mineral tsumoite (Te: white, soft, with polishing scratches), enclosed by chlorite (black), pyrrhotite (brown) containing pentlandite (light yellow "flames"), and chalcopyrite (brassy yellow with polishing scratches). Specimen 96-6 (Watkinson, 1999) collected from contact area of Ni-Cu-PGE ore and metasedimentary rocks of the McKim Formation, Copper Cliff South deposit, Sudbury. Submitted by D.H. Watkinson and D. Marshall.

spy 1

spy 2

Sphalerite (sph)

Environment: SEDEX, MVT, VMS
epithermal, vein, skarn

ZnS   **Cubic**

Characteristics

Hand Specimen	
Colour	White, yellow, brown, black - darkening with increased Fe
Hardness	3.5 – 4
Density	3.9 – 4.1

Polished Section			
Colour	Grey	Cleavage	{011} Perfect
Bireflectance	Not present	Anisotropy	Isotropic
Refl (546nm)	16.6	Refl (589nm)	16.4

Distinguishing Features

Sphalerite can be extremely variable in colour in hand specimen, but is distinguished by its resinous lustre (though may be earthy to submetallic when in colliform or massive habits), tetrahedral or dodecahedral crystals, often twinned, pale brown to yellow to colourless streak, perfect cleavage (in 6 directions), and low hardness. The dark (Fe-rich) end member is called "blackjack", and the white end member is often overlooked in hand specimen. In polished section, the grey colour, isotropism, and abundant yellow-brown to reddish brown internal reflections are characteristic. Also, it generally takes a good polish, has low reflectance, and lamellar twinning is sometimes observed in polished sections.

Associated Minerals

Galena, pyrite, marcasite, chalcopyrite, pyrrhotite, arsenopyrite, fluorite, and tetrahedrite in all types of sulphide deposits.

Mode of Occurrence

A common mineral, sphalerite is the major ore of zinc and occurs in many types of ore deposits, where it is typically associated with galena. It may occur as euhedral to subhedral crystals, as disseminated grains, as irregular anhedral masses with other sulphides, and as colloform-banded material with galena. In MVT deposits, sphalerite is associated with galena, marcasite, chalcopyrite, calcite, and dolomite. In VMS and SEDEX deposits, sphalerite is a major ore mineral with galena and chalcopyrite. Sphalerite also occurs in veins and in contact metamorphic deposits. The high-temperature polymorph of ZnS is wurtzite, which is hexagonal.

References

Fowler A.D. (1996) Self-organized banded sphalerite and branching galena in the Pine Point ore deposit, Northwest Territories. Canadian Mineralogist, v. 34, p. 1211-1222.

Kucha H. and Wieczorek A. (1984) Sulfide - carbonate relationships in the Navan (Tara) Zn-Pb Deposit, Ireland. Mineralium Deposita, v. 19, p. 208-216.

Lentz D.R. (2002) Sphalerite and arsenopyrite at the Brunswick No. 12 massive-sulfide deposit, Bathurst Camp, New Brunswick: Constraints on P-T evolution. Canadian Mineralogist, v. 40, p. 19-31.

Logan M.A.V. (2000) Mineralogy and geochemistry of the Gualilán skarn deposit in the Precordillera of western Argentina. Ore Geology Reviews, v. 17, p. 113-138.

Mizuta T. and Scott S.D. (1997) Kinetics of iron depletion near pyrrhotite and chalcopyrite inclusions in sphalerite: The sphalerite speedometer. Economic Geology, v. 92, p. 772-783.

Scott S.D. (1976) Application of the sphalerite geobarometer to regionally metamorphosed terrains. American Mineralogist, v. 61, p. 661-670.

Figures

sph 1 Breccia fragments replaced by greenish sphalerite and rimmed and cut by orange sphalerite. Matrix is magnesite. Specimen from Gayna River, Northwest Territories. Simon Fraser University collection. Photograph by Dan Marshall.

sph 2 Drusy sphalerite (brown) followed by quartz (white) in a vein cutting brecciated Nelson granodiorite. Entreprise deposit, Kokanee Range, British Columbia. Submitted by Georges Beaudoin, Université Laval.

sph 3 Alternating zones of iron-rich (dark brown) and iron-poor (yellow) sphalerite in vein (doubly polished thin section). Silvana deposit, Kokanee Range, British Columbia. Submitted by Georges Beaudoin, Université Laval.

sph 4 Chalcopyrite (yellow) and pyrrhotite (white) cross cutting and replacing sphalerite (grey). Gangue minerals are quartz (hexagon) and calcite. Simon Fraser University collection. Plane polarized reflected light. Photograph by Dan Marshall.

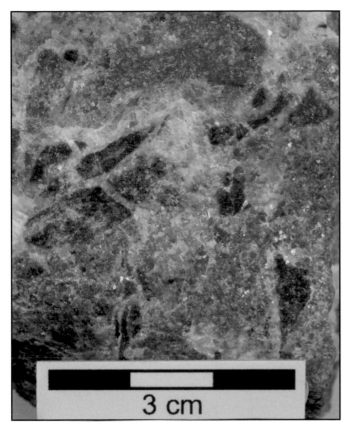

sph 1

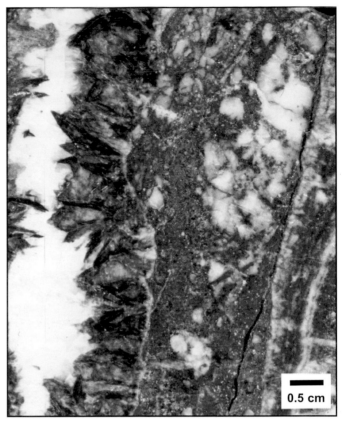

sph 2

sph 3

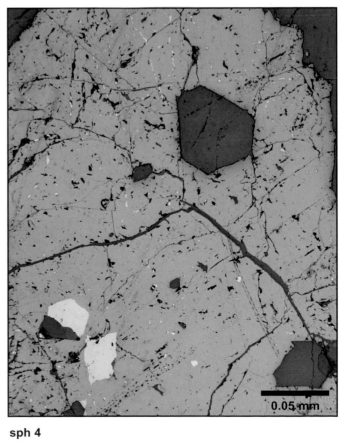

sph 4

Stibnite (stb)

Environment: Epithermal, VMS, mesothermal, SEDEX

Sb$_2$S$_3$

Orthorhombic

Characteristics

Hand Specimen	
Colour	Lead grey to black
Hardness	2
Density	4.5 – 4.6

Polished Section			
Colour	White to smokey grey	Cleavage	{010} Perfect
Bireflectance	Strong, white to grey-white	Anisotropy	Very strong, blue, grey, brown, pinkish
Refl (546nm)	32.3 – 47.8	Refl (589nm)	30.9 – 45.0

Distinguishing Features

In hand specimen, the colour and streak are lead grey to black, with metallic lustre. Stibnite commonly forms prismatic crystals, some curving or with longitudinal striations. Cleavage is perfect and parallel to the elongation direction. Small pieces will melt in a flame, yielding a greenish blue colour. In polished section, the very low polishing hardness, strong bireflectance, very strong anisotropism, and undulatory extinction are characteristic. Deformed lamellar twins are also common.

Associated Minerals

Galena, Pb sulphosalts, cinnabar, pyrite, marcasite, chalcopyrite, arsenopyrite, realgar, orpiment, quartz, calcite, and gold.

Mode of Occurrence

Commonly forms radiating aggregates and may also occur as granular or compact masses. Stibnite occurs in low-temperature hydrothermal veins or replacement deposits and in hot spring deposits. Stibnite may occur in VMS deposits and as an accessory mineral in SEDEX and magmatic related deposits. Some of the world's richest deposits of stibnite are in the province of Hunan, China. Large radiating splays of stibnite crystals are found in late veins in the Giant Mine, NWT (see photo), and in vugs at Hemlo, Ontario.

References

Bailly L., Bouchot V., Beny C. and Milesi J-P. (2000) Fluid inclusion study of stibnite using infrared microscopy; an example from the Brouzils antimony deposit (Vendée, Armorican Massif, France). Economic Geology, v. 95, p. 221-226.

Fan D., Zhang T. and Ye J. (2003) The Xikuangshan Sb deposit hosted by the Upper Devonian black shale series, Hunan, China. Ore Geology Reviews, v. 24, p. 121-133.

Harris D.C. (1989) The Mineralogy and Geochemistry of the Hemlo Gold Deposit, Ontario. Geological Survey of Canada, Economic Geology Report 38, 88 p.

Munoz M., Courjault-Rade P. and Tollon F. (1992) The massive stibnite veins of the French Palaeozoic basement: A metallogenic marker of late Variscan brittle extension. Terra Nova, v. 4, p. 171-177.

Wagner T. and Cook N.J. (2000) Late-Variscan antimony mineralisation in the Rheinisches Schiefergebirge, NW Germany; evidence for stibnite precipitation by drastic cooling of high-temperature fluid systems. Mineralium Deposita, v. 35, p. 206-222.

Figures

stb 1 Stibnite with cinnabar from the Red Devil deposit, Alaska. Specimen S78.68 from Art Soregaroli. Photograph by Dan Marshall.

stb 2 Stibnite and dogtooth calcite. Hammer for scale, Giant deposit, Northwest Territories. Specimen DM2001-128 from Dan Marshall. Photograph by Laura Hubbard.

stb 3 Stibnite in polished thin section, plane polarized reflected light, showing the visible bireflectance.

stb 4 Corresponding photo under partially crossed polars. Note the very strong anisotropy, deep blue and reddish brown. Simon Fraser University collection. Photograph by Dan Marshall.

stb 1

stb 2

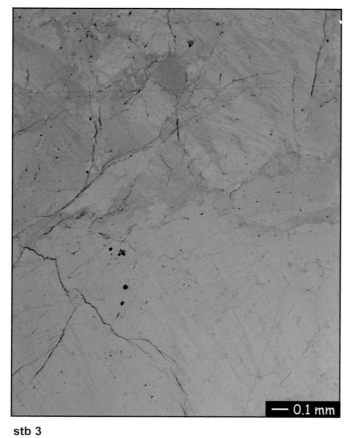

stb 3

stb 4

Tetrahedrite - Tennantite (td-tn)

Environment: Epithermal
VMS, SEDEX

$Cu_{12}SbS_{13}$ - $Cu_{12}As_4S_{13}$

Cubic

Characteristics
Tetrahedrite (td)

Hand Specimen	
Colour	Steel grey to black
Hardness	3 – 4
Density	4.5 – 5.2

Polished Section			
Colour	Grey, olive or brownish tint	Cleavage	Absent
Bireflectance	Not present	Anisotropy	Isotropic
Refl (546nm)	32.8	Refl (589nm)	32.7

Tennantite (tn)

Hand Specimen	
Colour	Steel grey with cherry red tint
Hardness	3 – 4
Density	4.6 – 4.7

Polished Section			
Colour	Grey, green or blue tint	Cleavage	Absent
Bireflectance	Not present	Anisotropy	Isotropic
Refl (546nm)	28.3	Refl (589nm)	26.9

Distinguishing Features

In hand specimen, both minerals are black to steel grey, with a black to brown streak (tn may have a slight reddish tint to the streak), metallic lustre, tetrahedral crystal form, occasionally twinned, also massive and granular habits, and no cleavage. In polished section, tetrahedrite may show an olive or brown tint, whereas tennantite may have a bluish tint. The absence of bireflectance, moderate reflectance, isotropism, and good polish aid in identification. Growth zoning may be visible in thin section, especially in more As-rich members (tn), and red internal reflections (IR) may be seen in tennantite (more abundant IR indicate greater amount of As).

Associated Minerals

Tetrahedrite forms a complete solid solution with tennantite. Associated minerals include sphalerite, galena, arsenopyrite, chalcopyrite, pyrite, silver minerals, and other sulphosalts.

Mode of Occurrence

Tetrahedrite is the most common of the sulphosalt group whereas tennantite is much more rare. Both minerals occur in low- to medium-temperature hydrothermal sulphide-bearing veins of copper, silver, lead, and zinc minerals. Tennantite usually occurs in a more As-rich environment. Tetrahedrite is also an important Ag-rich mineral in many deposits, such as at Broken Hill, Australia and Keno Hill, Yukon Territory. Tetrahedrite has also been reported in carbonatite, and in some VMS and SEDEX deposits.

References

Foit F.F. and Ulbricht M.E. (2001) Compositional variation in mercurian tetrahedrite-tennantite from the epithermal deposits of the Steens and Pueblo Mountains, Harney County, Oregon. Canadian Mineralogist, v. 39, p. 819-830.

Gaspar O.C. (2002) Mineralogy and sulfide mineral chemistry of the Neves Corvo ores, Portugal; insight into their genesis. Canadian Mineralogist, v. 40, p. 611-636.

Johnson N.E., Craig J.R. and Rimstidt J.D. (1988) Crystal chemistry of tetrahedrite. American Mineralogist, v. 73, p. 389-397.

King R.J. (2001) Minerals Explained 32: The tetrahedrite group. Geology Today, v. 17, p. 77-80.

Lynch J.V.G. (1989) Large-scale hydrothermal zoning reflected in the tetrahedrite-freibergite solid solution, Keno Hill, Ag-Pb-Zn district, Yukon. Canadian Mineralogist, v. 27, p. 383-400.

Figures

td-tn 1 Tetrahedrite crystals on dolomite. Cavnic, Romania. F.O.V. 6 cm. Submitted by Musée de géologie Réne-Bureau. Photograph by Georges Beaudoin, Université Laval.

td-tn 2 Silver-rich tennantite in siderite gangue from the Friday deposit, Coeur d'Alene district, Idaho. Specimen from Art Soregaroli. Photograph by Dan Marshall.

td-tn 3 Galena (gn) and pyrite (py) surrounded by tetrahedrite-tennantite (td-tn) in a quartz (qtz) matrix. Midway deposit, British Columbia. F.O.V. 2.5 mm. Submitted by Georges Beaudoin, Université Laval.

td-tn 4 Pyrite (py) replaced by tennantite (tn) and chalcopyrite (cp). There are also minor amounts of covellite developed on tennantite. All in quartz (qtz) vein. Reflected light. Teck Cominco specimen R94:1941.

td-tn 1

td-tn 2

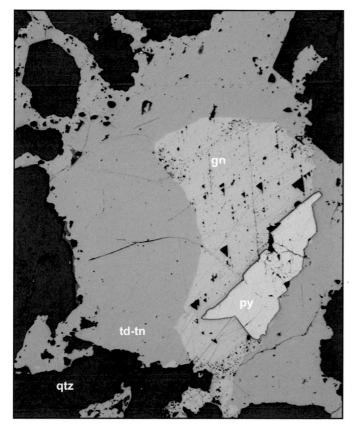

td-tn 3

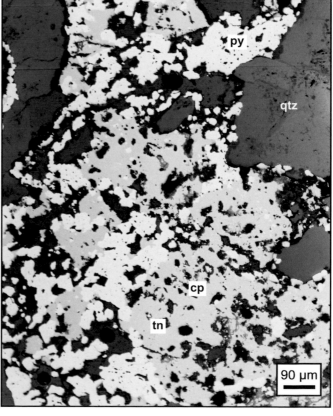

td-tn 4

Uraninite (ur)

Environment: Magmatic, placer, epithermal, pegmatite, sedimentary

UO_2

Cubic

Characteristics

Hand Specimen	
Colour	Black to brownish black
Hardness	5 – 6
Density	7.5 – 9.7

Polished Section			
Colour	Brownish grey	**Cleavage**	{111} Imperfect
Bireflectance	Absent	**Anisotropy**	Isotropic
Refl (546nm)	16.0	**Refl (589nm)**	15.8

Distinguishing Features

In hand specimen, uraninite is black to brownish black, with a similar coloured streak. The lustre varies from submetallic to greasy or dull depending on the habit, which can vary from massive (commonly referred to as pitchblende) to botryoidal or granular, and may also include cubic, octahedral, or dodecahedral crystals. In polished section, it is characterized by dark brown internal reflections, isotropism, and brownish grey colour (low reflectance). It is commonly zoned. Uraninite is strongly radioactive and the radioactivity commonly creates "radioactive haloes" in adjacent minerals.

Associated Minerals

Uranophane, brannerite, coffinite, molybdenite, bismuth, galena, fluorite, pyrite, Cu-Fe sulphides, Cu-Ni arsenides, vanadates, native silver, and gold.

Mode of Occurrence

Occurs as crystals in granite and syenite pegmatite, in masses and colloform crusts in high-temperature hydrothermal sulphide veins, as clastic grains in quartz-pebble conglomerate (e.g. Elliot Lake, Ontario), and as massive, colloform, and botryoidal pitchblende in unconformity-related hydrothermal deposits (e.g. Athabasca Basin, Saskatchewan).

References

England G.L., Rasmussen B., Krapez B. and Groves D.I. (2001) The origin of uraninite, bitumen nodules, and carbon seams in Witwatersrand gold-uranium-pyrite ore deposits, based on a Permo-Triassic analogue. Economic Geology, v. 96, p. 1907-1920.

Fayek M., Harrison T.M., Grove M. and Coath C.D. (2000) A rapid in situ method for determining the ages of uranium oxide minerals: Evolution of the Cigar Lake deposit, Athabasca Basin. International Geology Review, v. 42, p. 163-171.

Korzeb S.L., Foord E.E. and Lichte F.E. (1997) The chemical evolution and paragenesis of uranium minerals from the Ruggles and Palermo granitic pegmatites, New Hampshire. Canadian Mineralogist, v. 35, p. 135-144.

Min M.Z., Luo X.Z., Du G.S., He B.A. and Campbell A.R. (1999) Mineralogical and geochemical constraints on the genesis of the granite-hosted Huangao uranium deposit, SE China. Ore Geology Reviews, v. 14, p. 105-127.

Min M.Z., Luo X.Z., Mao S.L., Wang Z.Q., Wang R.C., Qin L.F. and Tan X.L. (2001) An excellent fossil wood cell texture with primary uranium minerals at a sandstone-hosted roll-type uranium deposit, NW China. Ore Geology Reviews, v. 17, p. 233-239.

Figures

ur 1   Uraninite crystal from the Cardiff deposit, Wilberforce, Ontario. The edge of the coin is 1.9 cm. Specimen W473 from the Wank collection. Photograph by Dan Marshall.

ur 2   Typical black massive uraninite (pitchblende) from the Ranwick Uranium deposit, Montreal River, Algoma District, Canada. Photograph is 4 cm across. Photograph by Mark Mauthner.

ur 3   Photomicrograph of brown-grey uraninite with light grey uranophane overgrowths (location unknown). Plane reflected light. F.O.V. 1.4 mm x 1.7 mm. Submitted by C.G. Couëslan and A.H. Mumin, Brandon University, Manitoba.

ur 4   Photomicrograph of **ur 3** in reflected light with crossed polars. Uraninite is dark brown-grey, uranophane is light orange.

ur 1

ur 2

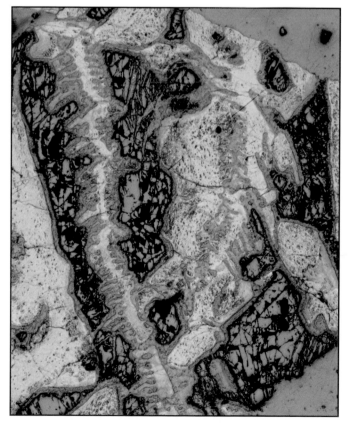

ur 3

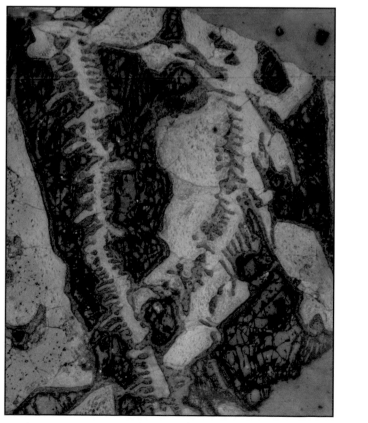

ur 4

Violarite (vio)

Environment: Secondary, magmatic, metamorphic

$FeNi_2S_4$

Cubic

Characteristics

Distinguishing Features

The purplish or violet-grey colour is characteristic in hand specimen. It has a metallic lustre, though violarite tarnishes readily, and has perfect cubic cleavage. In polished section, violarite is also violet-grey, isotropic, and typically displays a "crackly" or porous texture, and cubic cleavage. Its distinct colour in polished section makes it readily distinguishable from pyrite.

Hand Specimen	
Colour	Metallic violet grey
Hardness	4½ – 5½
Density	4.5 – 4.8

Polished Section			
Colour	Brownish grey with purple tint	Cleavage	{001} Perfect
Bireflectance	Not present	Anisotropy	Isotropic
Refl (546nm)	42.7	Refl (589nm)	44.0

Associated Minerals

Occurs as a supergene modification of Ni ores. Associated with millerite, pentlandite, chalcopyrite, cubanite, Ni-Co arsenides, pyrrhotite, and pyrite.

Mode of Occurrence

A member of the linnaeite group of minerals (Co-Cu-Ni-Fe sulphides), violarite most commonly occurs as an alteration product. It is found along grain boundaries and fractures in pentlandite, pyrrhotite, chalcopyrite, and millerite. Violarite is found at the Vermillion deposit, near Sudbury, Ontario (this deposit is the type locality for violarite) and in many other Ni-bearing ores.

References

Grguric B.A. (2002) Hypogene violarite of exsolution origin from Mount Keith, Western Australia field evidence for a stable pentlandite-violarite tie line. Mineralogical Magazine, v. 62, p. 313-326.

Misra K.C. and Fleet M.E. (1974) Chemical composition and stability of violarite. Economic Geology, v. 69, p. 391-403.

Patterson G.C. and Watkinson D.H. (1984) Metamorphism and supergene alteration of Cu-Ni sulfides, Thierry Mine, northwestern Ontario. *in* Ore Deposits and Related Petrology of Mafic-Ultramafic Suites. Canadian Mineralogist, v. 22, p. 13-21.

Richardson S. and Vaughan D.J. (1989) Surface alteration of pentlandite and spectroscopic evidence for secondary violarite formation. Mineralogical Magazine, v. 53, p. 213-222.

Figures

vio 1 Violarite with pyrrhotite from the Vermilion deposit, Sudbury, Ontario. Coin diameter is 1.9 cm. Specimen from Lloyd Twaits. Photograph by Dan Marshall.

vio 2 Pentlandite (centre) replaced by "crackly" violarite in contact with pyrrhotite (po). Blue Lake, Quebec. F.O.V. 0.3 mm. Submitted by Georges Beaudoin, Université Laval.

vio 3 Violarite replacing yellowish pentlandite along crystal boundaries of pyrrhotite (po). Black phases are silicate non-opaque gangue minerals. Plane polarized reflected light. Sample contributed by Nicki McKay, SGS-Lakefield Research Limited. Photograph by Dan Marshall.

vio 1

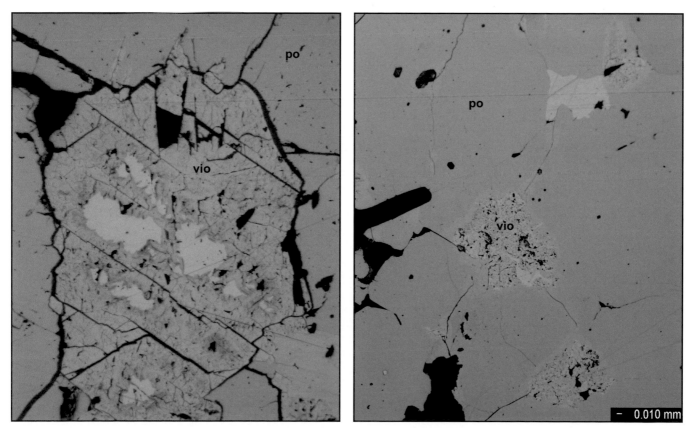

vio 2

vio 3

Wolframite (wf)

Environment: Pegmatite, vein, magmatic, porphyry

(Fe,Mn)WO₄

$(Fe,Mn)WO_4$

Monoclinic

Characteristics

Hand Specimen	
Colour	Dark brown to black
Hardness	4½ – 5½
Density	7.0 – 7.5

Polished Section			
Colour	Light grey to white	**Cleavage**	{010} Distinct
Bireflectance	Weak	**Anisotropy**	Distinct: grey-yellow
Refl (546nm)	15.0 – 17.0	**Refl (589nm)**	14.9 – 16.9

Distinguishing Features

Wolframite has a black to grey or brown colour, with a reddish brown to brownish black streak, submetallic to resinous lustre, perfect cleavage in one direction, and is translucent to opaque. It occurs as tabular or prismatic crystals elongated along the c-axis and commonly twinned. It also occurs as lamellar masses. The relatively high density, colour, lustre, cleavage, and crystal habit are characteristic. Some varieties can be slightly magnetic. In polished section, wolframite takes a good polish, and internal reflections are usually seen in red, brown, and/or yellow-brown, cleavage is distinct, and twinning common. Wolframite has oblique extinction, and occurs as tabular euhedral crystals or irregular grains. The lamellar form, oblique extinction, internal reflections, and low reflectance are characteristic.

Associated Minerals

Cassiterite, scheelite, hematite, arsenopyrite, pyrite, chalcopyrite, sphalerite, molybdenite, bismuth, bismuthinite, and gold.

Mode of Occurrence

Wolframite occurs in veins, and pegmatite mineralization, related to granite, granitic pegmatite and greisen, e.g. Sn-Cu vein deposits in Cornwall, England; W-Sn veins at Panasqueira, Portugal; vein stockwork and greisen Sn and W at Mount Pleasant, New Brunswick; and Climax-type Mo-porphyry deposits.

References

Foxford K. A., Nicholson R. and Polya D. A. (1991) Textural evolution of W-Cu-Sn-bearing hydrothermal veins at Minas da Panasqueira, Portugal. Mineralogical Magazine, v. 55, p. 435-445.

Lu H-Z., Liu Y., Wang C., Xu Y. and Li H. (2003) Mineralization and fluid inclusion study of the Shizhuyuan W-Sn-Bi-Mo-F skarn deposit, Hunan Province, China. Economic Geology, v. 98, p. 995-974.

Schmitz C. and Burt D.M. (1990). The Black Pearl Mine, Arizona; Wolframite veins and stockscheider pegmatite related to an albitic stock. Geological Society of America, Special Paper 246, p. 221-232.

Figures

wf 1 Vein sample of wolframite (black), quartz and potassic feldspar (pink). The sample is from a (quartz-wolframite-loellingite) sheeted greisen fracture system. The veins formed in extensional fractures or shear-extension hybrid fractures. The linear features are attributed to seismic-hydraulic fracturing. The W mineralization is part of the early high-temperature lodes of the Cornubian orefield. North Pool Zone, South Crofty deposit, southwest England. Photograph by Alan Anderson, St. Francis Xavier University.

wf 2 Wolframite in massive quartz vein. Fiddler Property, Yukon. Specimen S64:27 from Art Soregaroli. Photograph by Dan Marshall.

wf 3 Massive wolframite with minor gangue in fractures. Yaogangxian, Hunan, China. Plane polarized reflected light. Specimen from Jacob Hanley, University of Toronto. Photograph by Dan Marshall.

wf 4 Corresponding microphotograph taken under partly crossed polars showing the distinctive grey to purplish brown anisotropic colours, and delineating the silicate gangue in the fractures.

wf 1

wf 2

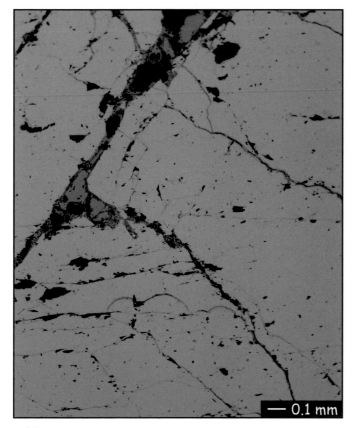

— 0.1 mm

wf 3

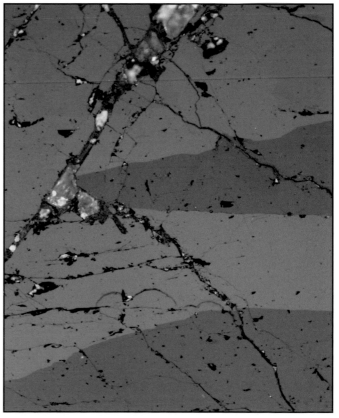

wf 4

MINERAL INDEX

Mineral Index Continued

Mineral Index Continued

Mineral Index Continued